A Third Way

A Third Way

Conversations About Anabaptist/Mennonite Faith

PAUL M. LEDERACH

Introduction by
George R. Brunk, III

HERALD PRESS
Scottdale, Pennsylvania
Kitchener, Ontario
1980

Library of Congress Cataloging in Publication Date

Lederach, Paul M
  A third way, conversations about Anabaptist/
Mennonite faith.

  Includes bibliographical references and index.
  1. Mennonites—Doctrinal and controversial works.
1. Title.
BX8121.2.L43   230.973   80-18041
ISBN 0-8361-1934-7 (pbk.)

A THIRD WAY
Copyright © 1980 by Herald Press, Scottdale, Pa. 15683
  Published simultaneously in Canada by Herald Press,
  Kitchener, Ont. N2G 4M5
Library of Congress Catalog Card Number: 80-18041
International Standard Book Number: 0-8361-1934-7
Printed in the United States of America
Design: Alice B. Shetler

15 14 13 12 11 10 9 8 7 6 5 4 3 2 1

This book is dedicated
to the children in our biological family
James, Judith, Deborah, and Rebecca
with the hope
that as they are confronted
by many beliefs and theological streams
they will continue to take their place
in the spiritual family
that bears the name
Anabaptist/Mennonite.

Contents

Introduction

Guard the truth! This instruction of the Apostle Paul to the young Timothy is always applicable to Christian believers. A treasury of truth has been entrusted to us—a pearl of great price, to use the words of Jesus. The story of God's action for the salvation of the world is not a common commodity of human knowledge that could be reacquired if once lost. The good news is revelation to a particular people in a particular time, which is preserved only by being remembered, either in the mind or in memory "banks" such as written Scripture. As has been said, "We are always only one generation away from losing the Christian faith."

It is also true that the gospel calls to a way of life that runs counter to the natural flow of human life. Christians are "up-stream" people. They cannot depend on the normal processes of society to reinforce their ideas. Because of settled convictions about the ideals of life, they dare not simply accept (as the majority does) whatever culture concocts. They must protect and promote their faith with unusual effort and constant attention. Guard the truth!

But even guarding a priceless pearl has its perils! A vivid parable I once read expressed the danger this way. A certain family wanting to protect a heirloom pearl placed it in a safe box. Only once a year would they open the box to gaze at the pearl. Gradually they decorated the box with costly jewels to compensate for the hidden beauty of the pearl. As a consequence the pearl was less appreciated than the box. Finally, the annual opening of the box was stopped. But it wasn't long before the young generation, who had never seen the pearl, began to doubt if there really was a pearl at all! So, preserving the faith by hedging it about with accumulated cultural trappings can really destroy true faith. Guarding the truth is more like caring for a garden that needs cultivation to be kept alive. Guard the truth!

Paul M. Lederach has done us a particular service in showing how to preserve our heritage of faith with integrity and faithfulness. It was my privilege to serve with the author in the formulation of the statement, *Affirming Our Faith in Word and Deed,* on which this book is based (see Appendix). The strengths which he brought to that task are evident here. One is impressed by the breadth of biblical knowledge which is brought to bear on the points of discussion. There is also a depth of conviction which emerges from the lines—a conviction, however, that reflects neither bitterness nor narrowness toward the objects of criticism. Lastly, one can appreciate the simple communication of profound insights. Recent writing on the Anabaptist "third way" has been predominantly for scholars. Here the findings of the scholars are communicated by one who has dedicated long years to educating the church in its faith.

I am confident that this book can challenge the church to "lengthen the cords and strengthen the stakes" (Isaiah 54:2) of that kingdom whose primacy is here proclaimed. My hope is that it will help both those of "the third way" and those of other ways to greater conformity to Him who is *the* way.

George R. Brunk, III, Dean
Eastern Mennonite Seminary
Harrisonburg, Virginia

Author's Preface

This book has a dual purpose. First it is an attempt to set forth in simple terms some of the key affirmations of the Mennonite faith. In this I was guided by *Affirming Our Faith in Word and Deed*, the statement (see Appendix) and study guide recommended by the Mennonite Church General Assembly in 1977 for congregational study and response. In a general way this book follows the divisions of the study guide. Second, I have tried to compare or to contrast Anabaptist/Mennonite views with other theological streams, both historical and current.

It is in the second area that I feel I am most often on slippery ground. It is difficult to express clearly and honestly the views of others that diverge from one's own. However, such comparisons and contrasts are much needed today. Many writers have set forth what they perceive to be Anabaptist/ Mennonite views. But rarely are these views placed side by side with other views. As a consequence, the "third way" of Mennonite faith is often unnoticed even by those who bear the name. For many the Mennonite faith is simply a form of evangelicalism or even Fundamentalism with a few special emphases like nonresistance and nonconformity tacked on. They are unaware of the radical departure Mennonite faith takes from commonly held notions about how Jesus is central, the nature of the kingdom, the nature of the church, and the nature of salvation.

This book began as a series of sermons preached at the Mennonite Church of Scottdale (Pa.). Invitations to share the substance of these sermons in other contexts led to the decision to prepare the material in book form.

Personally, I was hesitant to prepare this book. I sense my own limitations in theological backgrounds both of my own Mennonite tradition and those I attempt to compare. I am sure there are many points along the way that will make persons within the Mennonite stream and outside of it unhappy. Nevertheless, I have a deep sense that something like this is needed. I hope that the inadequacies of this book will encourage those more qualified to prepare a more definitive work.

To contrast and to compare one's faith with others runs many risks. For one, there is the tendency to caricature the faith of others to make the point. Another is to state one's position as though it were right and the other wrong. I have tried to avoid both, but confess I have not fully succeeded. I hope, however, that this book will lead to discussion both within the Mennonite stream and with those in other theological streams.

Though vocabulary words are similar, yet meanings vary widely. Perhaps it is in the wisdom of God that there are many theological streams, so that in the end the totality of His truth will be comprehended in ways no one stream could communicate alone. Thus a responsibility is placed upon each stream to articulate and to live its vision as clearly as possible. It is my opinion that those in the Anabaptist/ Mennonite stream make their best contribution to the total Christian community when, lovingly, they articulate clearly and live committedly the vision that has come to them. When this is done with respect for others, the confluence of these streams will result in new learnings, new commitments, and new forms of obedience for these times. And the truth of God in its varicolored splendor will be seen and known in the world.

"May the God of steadfastness and encouragement grant you to live in such harmony with one another, in accord with Christ Jesus, that together you may with one voice glorify the God and Father of our Lord Jesus Christ" (Romans 15:5, 6).

Paul M. Lederach
June, 1979

4 BC - 32 AD	Life of Christ
32 - 62 AD	Pauline Epistles written
62 - 99 AD	Gospels of Mark, Matthew, Luke
96 - 128 AD	Rest of New Testament written (except for II Peter which was later)

CHAPTER 1

The Centrality of Jesus Christ

There are many theological traditions within the bosom of Christianity. As each tradition examines its faith and contrasts it with other theological positions, feelings of superiority and arrogance, or notions that "we have the truth," while others do not, must be avoided. Rather, with humility believers should attempt to perceive the shape of their faith, with the hope that among all of the voices today, they will be able to make a clear witness to their faith. The purpose of this volume is to put into the conversation some perspectives from the Mennonite/Anabaptist theological tradition.

The words used by the various theological streams are the same. But each stream tends to pour different meanings into these words. Most theological positions—whether Lutheran, Reformed, Anabaptist, Fundamentalist, or Dispensational— agree that "Jesus Christ is central." How He is made central, however, seems to differ greatly.

Before discussing these perspectives, a word should be said about the Bible. This study will not enter into questions of Bible interpretation as such. At the expense of oversimplification, it seems that the various theological streams result from starting at different places in interpreting the Bible. Where one begins has a strong bearing on where one ends!*

Some theological positions seem to begin with the Old Testament. Here the Old Testament and the New Testament are seen as equally authoritative. Jesus and the church are merely a continuation of the story of Israel or an interval before God works with Israel again. The Old Testament provides the base for practices in the New Testament church. For example, infant baptism is based on the Old Testament, where males were circumcised to symbolize their entrance into the covenant community. In a similar way the baptism of infants establishes a covenant relationship within the people of God, the church.

Other theological positions seem to begin with the New Testament. Here the New Testament is seen as God's final and full revelation. The Old Testament is interpreted in the light of the New. But this also creates a problem. Does the interpretation begin with Paul and the epistles? Does it begin with Jesus and the Gospels? Some traditions seem to begin with the Apostle Paul, and everything is interpreted from the stance of the apostle and his writings. Luther came to his tremendous discovery in the writings of Paul, that the just live by faith. Consequently, Luther focused primarily on the cross, and on justification—guilt is removed.

Others began with Jesus and the Gospels. All the Scrip-

---

*"To begin" is perhaps too simple a way to deal with a difficult and complex problem of Bible interpretation. It refers to presuppositions. Implicitly it also takes into account the history of interpretation—pre-critical interpretation (early and medieval church), transition to critical (Reformation), critical (19th, 20th century), post-critical (coming of psychoanalytical approaches), and the degree to which these are involved and normative in the theological traditions.

tures are interpreted from the standpoint of Jesus as He is
portrayed in the Gospels. Both the Old Testament and the
rest of the New Testament are interpreted from the Gospels.
The Old Testament points to Jesus Christ. The letters of
Paul and other epistles find their meaning in the person of
Jesus, found in the Gospels.

At the risk of oversimplification, the Mennonite/
Anabaptist theological stream began with Jesus and the Gospels. Jesus' life and teachings were of extreme importance.
They were not, however, separated from His death and
resurrection!

The Apostles' Creed illustrates a way in which Jesus is
made central.

> I believe in God the Father Almighty, maker of heaven and
> earth: and in Jesus Christ His only Son our Lord, who was
> conceived by the Holy Spirit, born of the Virgin Mary, suffered
> under Pontius Pilate, was crucified, dead, and buried. He
> descended into hell; the third day He arose again from the
> dead. He ascended into heaven, and sitteth on the right hand of
> God the Father Almighty; from thence He shall come to judge
> the quick and the dead. I believe in the Holy Spirit; the holy
> catholic church; the communion of saints; the forgiveness of
> sins; the resurrection of the body; and the body everlasting.
> Amen.

The Mennonite/Anabaptist theological stream does not
deny the truth of the creed. It simply says it doesn't go far
enough! Why? Between "born of the Virgin Mary" and
"suffered under Pontius Pilate" the *life, work, and teachings
of Jesus are ignored!* For many theological traditions, to
make Jesus central is to focus on His virgin birth, or on the
cross, or on His return—as important as these matters are.
The failure is to take seriously the thrust of the Gospels, that
God has come in the flesh, in the person of Jesus of Naza-

reth, and consequently His life and teachings are exceedingly important. What is done with the life and teachings of Jesus creates a watershed in how Jesus is made central.

Mennonite/Anabaptist theology acknowledges the importance of the cross, the resurrection, the ascension, and the return. But the stress is on the resurrection. The earliest confession of faith, Schleitheim, speaks of *walking in the resurrection*, which brings together both the *pattern* and the *power* Jesus provides.

To make Jesus central, six things should be stressed.

1. *God has come in the person of Jesus.* Therefore Jesus is the clearest revelation of what God is like. Humans want to know about God. The many religious and worship practices among all peoples, on all continents and islands of the sea, illustrate this search to know God. Mennonites, as well as other Christians, share the belief that Jesus provides a clear revelation of what God is like. John wrote, "No one has ever seen God; the only Son, who is in the bosom of the Father, he has made him known" (John 1:18). Jesus said to Philip, "He who has seen me has seen the Father" (John 14:9). Paul wrote the same thing, "For it is the God who said, 'Let light shine out of darkness' [that is the God of creation] who has shone in our hearts to give the light of knowledge of the glory of God in the face of Christ!" (2 Corinthians 4:6).

The great preacher of the New Testament began his sermon thus: "In many and various ways God spoke of old to our fathers by the prophets; but in these last days he has spoken to us by a Son, whom he appointed the heir of all things, through whom also he created the world. He reflects the glory of God and bears the very stamp of his nature, upholding the universe by his word of power" (Hebrews 1:1-3).

2. *Jesus is the clearest revelation of what God intends*

human beings to be like. This is not emphasized as much as
the first point. But it is at home in Mennonite faith that underscores the importance of the life and teachings of Jesus.
Paul wrote that believers are to be conformed to the image
of His Son: "For those whom he foreknew he also
predestined to be conformed to the image of his Son in order
that he might be the first-born among many brethren"
(Romans 8:29).

Today there is renewed emphasis on new birth. This has
been a fundamental belief of the believers' church since its
beginning. However, it is important to realize that the words
"follow me" appear more frequently in the New Testament
than "born again." (Born again appears in John's Gospel, 1
Peter, and in 1 John.) The importance of this has not
dawned on much of North American Christendom.

John's Gospel, in which the concept "born anew" is
found, begins with the call to follow. Jesus found Philip and
said, "Follow me" (John 1:43). It ends as the disciples sur-
rounded the risen Lord. His last words to Peter and John
were "Follow me" (John 21:19, 22).

Check a concordance for the word "follow." Look up the
references in the Gospels. At least two times in each of the
Synoptic Gospels Jesus spoke of taking up the cross and
following. Again, in the Gospel of John, Jesus said that those
who *follow* Him will not walk in darkness (John 8:12). He
also used the figure of the shepherd and the sheep. Jesus saw
His followers as sheep following a shepherd. "I know them,"
He said, "and they follow me" (John 10:27). In Jesus' final
public sermon, He said, "If any one serves me, he must
follow me" (John 12:26).

Believers are to follow Jesus, because He is the revelation
of how God intended people to be! This insight has been a
historical Mennonite emphasis. Only recently have Men-

nonites embraced other traditions which focus largely on Jesus' cross at the expense of His life and teaching. To emphasize His life and teaching is not to minimize grace, for as Paul wrote, "God is at work in you, both to will and to work for his good pleasure" (Philippians 2:13).

Hans Denck lived from 1500 to 1527. (It's amazing how many Anabaptist leaders were very young and completely dedicated.) Because of his faith, Denck was banished from the city in which he lived and not allowed within ten miles of town. He was separated from his wife and young family. He died at the age of 27 from the plague. Denck was disturbed by what he saw going on. Among the Reformers, the doctrine of justification by faith seemed to guarantee the standing of a believer with God, regardless of the character of his life. However, Denck emphasized constantly the importance of following Jesus as a disciple. His motto has been heard across the centuries, "No one may truly know Christ except one who follows Him in life."°

3. *Jesus makes clear how God works in history.* The story the Bible tells climaxes in the coming of Jesus. Why did God call Abraham? Why did God call a people? Why did God have such patience with the people of Israel, narrow-minded and disobedient as they were? When the people were disobedient, they fell under the heel of oppressors. When they turned in repentance, God rescued them, and restored them. Why did God put up with such a people? Why was He so merciful and gracious?

An explanation is found in the prophet Isaiah. Isaiah 40 to 55 seems to refer to Israel, captive in Babylon. Israel's hopes were dashed. Then the prophet came with words of hope. Some of the people had nationalistic aspirations. They

---

° *Mennonite Encyclopedia*, Vol. 2, "Hans Denck," p. 33.

hoped for a restoration of a Davidic kingdom. But Isaiah saw something greater than a restoration of David's kingdom. Isaiah saw a suffering servant, one who would die for others, who would heal. For Israel, healing was much more than physical healing. To them healing meant salvation, room to move about, restoration.

Acts tells the story of the Ethiopian reading Isaiah as he traveled. He asked a messenger of God, "Of whom does Isaiah speak?" or "Who is the suffering servant?" (See Acts 8:34.) Then Philip explained that Isaiah's insight had its full development and final meaning in Jesus, the suffering servant. The past, the present, and the future of God's action are tied to the suffering servant. Jesus and His body, the church, make clear how and why God has worked in history!

4. *To make Jesus central is to be united with His church.* For many people salvation is simply a matter of intellectual belief. The gospel is reduced to several concise spiritual laws that are to be repeated and accepted. For them salvation turns out to be intellectual gymnastics. Salvation is called a "plan." But salvation is vastly more than a plan. It is a relationship. Salvation is very simple; yet, it is very complex. But one thing is clear—the New Testament intends for every person who comes to Jesus in faith to unite with His church. God never intended for a Christian to exist in isolation, sitting at home alone watching a TV church, or praying with his hand on the radio (unless one is an invalid or a shut-in).

Becoming a part of the church is not optional. And, as will be stressed later, there is no such thing as an invisible church, as though a saved person is part of a group that is not easily identifiable.

In the church the fullness of Jesus dwells (Ephesians 1:22, 23). Some theological streams, such as modern Dispensationalism, give little place for the church. The focus is on Israel, which it is thought will someday be restored. Thus there is great interest in Palestine and in international affairs. For the Dispensationalist the church is apostate anyway, a parenthesis between the time of Jesus and the time God restores Israel. Mennonite theology, however, focuses on what Jesus is doing now *in* the church, *for* the church, and *with* the church. For, as Paul wrote, Jesus is at God's "right hand in the heavenly places, far above all rule and authority and power and dominion, and above every name that is named, not only in this age but also in that which is to come, and he has put all things under his feet and has made him the head over all things for the church!" (Ephesians 1:20-22).

Again, Paul wrote, "To me, though I am the very least of all the saints, this grace was given, to preach to the Gentiles the unsearchable riches of Christ, and to make all men see what is the plan of the mystery hidden for ages in God, who created all things; that through the church the manifold wisdom of God might be made known" (Ephesians 3:8-10).

Jesus unites believers with His church. To be in the church is not optional. It's not a benefit offered on the side. The church is central because Jesus is central. The church is His body.

5. *The work of the Holy Spirit is experienced through Jesus.* The Spirit was sent by Jesus. The Spirit brings to mind what Jesus did and taught. When Jesus is central, believers judge all claims for the Spirit's work and presence by Jesus' life and teachings. Any claim for Spirit work or Spirit activity that in any way is not in harmony with the life and teaching of Jesus is judged for what it is—false. And at the same time, whenever lives demonstrate what it means to follow Jesus, this is the result of the work of the Holy Spirit.

6. *To make Jesus central is to be concerned for the salvation of the world.* Early Anabaptists expressed a concern for

the whole world. Long before the modern missionary movement, Detrich Phillip, an associate of Menno Simons, wrote about *sending* preachers and teachers. In fact, at the heart of Anabaptist/Mennonite faith was a missionary concern, a concern for the whole world. All persons are to come to know Jesus.

Isaiah implied this when he said to Israel that there is no God but Yahweh. If there is only one God, then there is the responsibility that the whole world come to know the one God. In the same way, to say, "Jesus is central," or "Jesus is Lord!" implies a missionary obligation! It means that the whole world must come to know the One who is central—who is Lord. Since there is one Lord, there can be no other. This is the scandal of Christianity. Christians firmly believe there is no other name under heaven given among men by which people are saved. Acts 4:12. A concern for the whole world motivated the early church—as Paul wrote to the Ephesians, grace was given him to preach to the Gentiles! Ephesians 3:8.

Thus Jesus is made central, when He reveals what God is like. Jesus is central when He makes clear what humans are to be like. Jesus is central when He provides the key for understanding how God is working in history. Jesus is central when He is acknowledged as Head of the church. Jesus is central when He is seen as the source of the Holy Spirit's work. Finally, Jesus is central when there is the concern that the whole world come to know Him.

CHAPTER 2

The Primacy of God's Kingdom

Where one begins in Bible interpretation influences the way the kingdom is understood. In the Anabaptist/Mennonite theological heritage, all of God's action is viewed from the standpoint of Jesus, especially His life and teachings.

A good place to begin thinking about the kingdom is in the Gospel of Matthew. There teachings about the kingdom are more fully developed than in other parts of the New Testament. Matthew includes the Sermon on the Mount. There Jesus taught, "Seek first the kingdom and its righteousness" (Matthew 6:33), which emphasized the primacy of the kingdom.

"Kingdom" appears about 50 times in Matthew, most frequently in the phrase "the kingdom of heaven". (In the original Greek, heaven is plural, and could be translated "the kingdom of heavens.")

Matthew also refers to "the kingdom of God" (12:28; 19: 23, 24; 21:31, 43). Some persons make a distinction between "the kingdom of heaven" and "the kingdom of

God." Likely, for Matthew and the rest of the New Testament writers, the terms were interchangeable. Matthew also refers to "the kingdom of the Son of Man" (13:41; 16:28). The kingdom is the Father's (6:10; 13:43; 26:29). The Lord's Prayer includes the words "Our Father, who art in heaven, hallowed be thy name. Thy kingdom come" — clearly the kingdom is also the Father's.

At times, a distinction seems to be made between "the kingdom of the Father" and "the kingdom of the Son" (13:41-43), since the kingdom of the Son of Man will be turned over to the Father, and the righteous will shine in the kingdom of the Father. Similarly, Paul wrote that Christ will deliver the kingdom to the Father after destroying every rule and every authority and power (1 Corinthians 15:24). If there is a distinction, it is likely a minor one, more in sequence than anything else.

Behind the idea of kingdom is the belief that Jesus is King! This is the meaning of the Great Confession, "Jesus is Lord!" Jesus is also called the "King of Israel" (John 1:49). In Galatians the church is called the Israel of God (6:16). Jesus is "the son of David" (Matthew 1:1), which has kingly implications. Jesus is also called "the Son of God (John 1:49). Often "Son of God" is said to refer to Jesus' divinity. However, the kings in Israel were often called sons of God (2 Samuel 7:14).

Thus the name Son of God, when applied to Jesus, spoke not only of His divinity but also of His kingship.

The name Jesus used for Himself most frequently was "Son of Man." The primary meaning of that name is king. It was said that "Son of Man" referred to His humanity, while "Son of God" referred to His divinity. However, both refer to royalty. Daniel 7:14 illustrates the royal implication of the name. Daniel wrote,

> I saw in the night visions,
> and behold, with the clouds of heaven
> there came one like a son of man,
> and he came to the Ancient of Days
> and was presented before him.
> And to him was given dominion and glory and kingdom,
> that all peoples, nations, and languages should serve him;
> his dominion is an everlasting dominion,
> which shall not pass away,
> and his kingdom one
> that shall not be destroyed.
>
> —Daniel 7:13, 14

The "Son of Man" appeared before the "Ancient of Days." In this passage also are terms that appear again in the New Testament:

(a) *"The clouds."* The "Son of Man" appeared with the clouds of heaven. This was replicated in Jesus' transfiguration.

(b) *"Dominion and glory."* In John's Gospel "glory" is frequently used in connection with Jesus—"We have beheld his glory, glory as of the only Son from the Father" (1:14).

(c) *"All peoples, nations, and languages."* The kingdom Daniel foresaw was universal, bringing together "all peoples, nations, and languages" to serve Him. This refrain appears in Revelation 5:9 and 7:9.

(d) *"Everlasting."* The kingdom of the "Son of Man" is eternal! Clearly, the name "Son of Man," which appears so frequently in Matthew and the other Gospels, speaks of a king and a kingdom!

Here are six observations about the kingdom.

1. *There are two kingdoms.* Paul wrote: "He [God] has delivered us from the *dominion of darkness* and transferred us to the *kingdom of his beloved Son* in whom we have redemption, the forgiveness of sins" (Colossians 1:13). There

are two kingdoms, the kingdom of God and the kingdom of darkness under the control of Satan.

In the story of Jesus' temptation, Satan came and offered Jesus all the kingdoms of this world. They were his to give (Matthew 4:8, 9). At this point it may be helpful to reflect on the phrase "a Christian nation." Is there such a thing as a Christian nation? Can any country of the world be labeled Christian? There are two kingdoms. There is the kingdom of God, the rule of God which is universal. And there are the kingdoms of this world. Clearly the kingdom of God does not know political or geographical boundaries!

Jesus said that His casting out demons was a sure sign that the kingdom had come (Matthew 12:28). When persons come to Jesus Christ, they receive new life. They become part of His body; they become part of His kingdom. Believers are children of His kingdom.

2. *What is the kingdom like?* Jesus described the kingdom through parables. Matthew contains many of these.

The kingdom is in the midst of conflict. Jesus illustrated this when He told about a man who owned a field. He sowed good seed but an enemy came and sowed weeds (13:24). The conflict is between the kingdom of God and the kingdom of Satan. Because of this conflict those who are citizens of the kingdom of God will suffer in the same way that Jesus suffered at the hands of the worldly kingdom. Those in the kingdom of God are despised by those in kingdoms of this world, and will be persecuted by them. This was clear to the Anabaptists. They recognized that their suffering was a result of the conflict between the two kingdoms.

The kingdom has a small beginning, but it will grow worldwide. Jesus told the story of the mustard seed to illustrate kingdom growth (13:31). He also spoke of yeast to illustrate how the kingdom grows (13:33). The kingdom does not move forward through political power or military might. Rather, the kingdom permeates—it moves through society like yeast moves through dough, until the whole is leavened.

The kingdom is of great value. Jesus told of a man who found a treasure in a field (13:44). In those days when there were no banks, people hid treasures to keep them safe. A man found a great sum of money in a field. He sold all that he had to purchase the field and obtain its treasure. In another story, a pearl merchant found a pearl of rare beauty and great size (13:45). He sold everything to buy that pearl.

The kingdom is a realm of forgiveness. Jesus told about a lord who forgave the debts of those who owed him money (18:23-35).

The kingdom is a realm of grace. The story Jesus told to illustrate this is hard for us to understand. A man hired a group of employees one morning to work in his vineyard (20:1-16). He offered a substantial wage for the day. At different times during the day, he hired additional persons to work in his vineyard. He offered the same wage to those who began work late in the day as to those he hired in the morning.

This cuts across our sense of justice. A man who works only one hour should receive less money than a man who works all day! But this is not the nature of God's grace. Why criticize what God does out of love and mercy? In His grace He gives as much to one as to another. Furthermore, His gracious gift is not dependent upon labor.

The kingdom requires sobriety and alertness. Christians are to be ready and watching (25:1-13).

This, then, is Jesus' view of the kingdom. It is in conflict. It grows. It penetrates. It is worldwide. It is the forgiving, gracious rule of God. Where God is present in saving power, where God is acknowledged, where God is obeyed, where God's will is being done—there is God's kingdom!

3. *Entrance into the kingdom.* When John the Baptist began preaching, he announced the coming kingdom, and called for repentance (3:1-3). When Jesus began preaching, He also announced that "the kingdom of heaven is at hand," and called for repentance (4:17).

Repentance is generally thought of as being sorry for sins. However, repentance is more than this. Repentance means to make a complete readjustment, or to reorient entirely one's life. Entrance into the kingdom requires a total change of life—a change of values, outlook, and allegiance. Kingdom citizens are new creatures with new loves and new directions. This change begins at the point of repentance.

4. *The kingdom is both present and future.* At conversion the believer moves from the domain of darkness into the kingdom of Christ. Every life that is redeemed, every body that is healed, every believer that experiences ongoing liberation from sin's bondage demonstrates that the power of the eventual, glorious, universal kingdom has entered the world now! The rule of God is even now undermining the authority of Satan and his kingdom, which is being replaced by the rule of God! Believers are experiencing now what will be.

Among the Anabaptists this idea was important. Right now the kingdom is here. Christians experience now a *foretaste* of what will be. If there will be love in the kingdom, there is love now. If there will be peace in the future kingdom, there is peace in the kingdom now. Those in the kingdom do not look forward to a time when swords will be beaten into plowshares, they are already demonstrating that reality. Kingdom people beat their swords into plowshares now! Clearly, peacemaking and nonresistance are basic to the gospel. Mennonite/Anabaptist theology is not simply "Protestant theology" with a few peculiar emphases tacked on. The Anabaptist view of the two kingdoms, and of the reality of the kingdom now as a foretaste of what will be, leads to a radical discipleship.

Anabaptist/Mennonite theology is also at odds with a theology popular among evangelicals, Dispensationalism. This theology emphasizes the kingdom, but the kingdom is almost totally future. Dispensationalism is modern from the standpoint of the history of Christian doctrine. It came on the scene about 150 years ago. J. N. Darby and a few others popularized the view. It has become the theology of most Bible institutes. Dispensationalism sees history divided into periods or dispensations. Jesus is seen as part of the dispensation of law, of the Old Testament. A church age will be followed by a kingdom age. The kingdom is separated from the church, and is altogether future. The church becomes a parenthesis between the dispensation of the law and the kingdom.

As a theology, Dispensationalism begins with the Old Testament, which becomes normative. Dispensationalists say that prophecies about the kingdom in the Old Testament have not been "literally" fulfilled, and, therefore, must be fulfilled in the future. They tend to skip over the work of Jesus, the life of Jesus, the ethics of Jesus, the kingdom in its present reality, and the church. This theology is quite far from Mennonite/Anabaptist understandings of the kingdom.

5. *Both the church and the kingdom are present realities.* God is working through the church today. The church and the kingdom are not separated. However, the church and the kingdom are not identical. The church is not the

kingdom, yet the church is inexplicably interwoven with the kingdom. The church proclaims the good news of the kingdom. The church is entrusted with the kingdom. Jesus said that the church is given the keys of the kingdom. Thus the church opens and closes the gates of the kingdom (Matthew 16:18, 19). The church has a responsibility to maintain the integrity of the fellowship under the rule of God.

The New Testament church/kingdom idea reflects the world in which New Testament Christians lived. Rome was the great kingdom. When Paul wrote his letter to Philippi, it was a colony of the Roman Empire. This illustrated the relationship between the church and the kingdom. There is a kingdom in which God rules from heaven. Each of the churches are colonies of the kingdom, on its frontiers. They are the local manifestations of the kingdom. The church does not build the kingdom nor does the church extend the kingdom. Rather, the work of the church is kingdom work. The churches are, as Paul wrote, central in God's plan for advancing His kingdom (Ephesians 3:10).

6. *Pentecost is pivotal for both the church and the kingdom.* For too many people salvation is a simple formula which, when accepted, leads to "being saved." A person's soul is saved by accepting these points. In this view Pentecost has meaning largely in an individualistic way. It leads to personal holiness, and is the root of charismatic experiences. A believer receives the gifts of the Holy Spirit which are expressed largely in an individual manner.

In the understanding of the kingdom outlined above, Pentecost takes a different turn. Pentecost is the fulfilling of all that had gone before. It fulfills the promises of Jesus. It brings into being a new people, who make up the body of Jesus Christ. The body has a head (a king), which is Jesus.

To the disciples Jesus "presented himself alive after his

passion by many proofs, appearing to them during forty days, and speaking of the kingdom of God. And while staying with them he charged them not to depart from Jerusalem, but to wait for the promise of the Father, which, he said, 'you heard from me, for John baptized with water, but before many days you shall be baptized with the Holy Spirit.'

"So when they had come together, they asked him, 'Lord, will you at this time restore the kingdom of Israel?' He said to them, 'It is not for you to know times or seasons which the Father has fixed by his own authority. But you shall receive power when the Holy Spirit has come upon you; and you shall be my witness in Jerusalem and in all Judea and Samaria and to the ends of the earth' " (Acts 1:3-8). Note that Jesus used the very same words that were said to Mary when Jesus was given a physical body—"The Holy Spirit will *come upon you,* and the power of the Most High will overshadow you (Luke 1:35). The power of God and of the Holy Spirit came to Mary to give Jesus a physical body. Jesus used the same words, "the Holy Spirit has *come upon you,*" to refer to the new body—the church. Thus at the heart of Pentecost is the creation of a new body, the body of Christ.

Pentecost is also the reversal of Babel. All of the stories in Genesis 1 through 11 end with a note of mercy. For example, after the flood was a rainbow. But at Babel there was no mercy. However, that's where the story of Abraham begins. God's mercy will be manifested in calling out a people!

As the Exodus created a people, so did Pentecost. In the Exodus, the people were led through the wilderness by a pillar of fire. At Pentecost there were tongues of fire. When the people came to the Red Sea, a mighty east wind opened the sea for them to pass through. At Pentecost there was also a sound of a mighty rushing wind! God was creating a new people! God was creating the body of Jesus Christ. At the head of the body is a Lord, a King, Jesus!

When Israel passed through the sea, Paul wrote, they were baptized into Moses (1 Corinthians 10:2). They were being made into a new people. Now listen to Peter's words at Pentecost. Note also the kingly language.

"Brethren, I may say to you confidently of the patriarch David that he both died and was buried, and his tomb was with us to this day. Being therefore a prophet, and knowing that God had sworn with an oath to him that he would set one of his descendants upon his throne, he foresaw and spoke of the resurrection of the Christ, that he was not abandoned to Hades, nor did his flesh see corruption. This Jesus God raised up, and of that we are all witnesses. Being therefore *exalted at the right hand of God* [this is the great enthronement!] and having received from the Father the promise of the Holy Spirit, he has poured out this which you see and hear. For David did not ascend into the heavens; but he himself says,

'The Lord said unto my Lord. Sit thou on my right hand, till I make thy enemies a stool for thy feet.'

"Let all the house of Israel therefore know assuredly that God has made Him both Lord and Christ, this Jesus whom you crucified."

Now when they heard this they were cut to the heart, and they said to Peter and the rest of the apostles, "Brethren, what shall we do?" And Peter said to them, "Repent, and be baptized [become part of the new people] every one of you in the name of Jesus Christ for the forgiveness of your sins; and you shall receive the gift of the Holy Spirit. For the promise is to you and your children and to all that are far off, every one whom the Lord our God calls to Him." And he testified with many other words and exhorted them, saying, "Save yourselves from this crooked generation" (Acts 2:29-40).

There are two kingdoms. Pentecost was the call to repentance, to leave the kingdom of darkness and to become part of the kingdom of God. The one whom God raised up is now at God's right hand!

Peter, therefore, called people to be baptized, to be saved from the crooked generation—the other kingdom. As the law given at Sinai made a new people, so Pentecost makes a new people under the rule of God. The kingdom is where the presence and the power of the Holy Spirit are manifested in the midst of a new people.

CHAPTER 3

The Visibility of the Church

The term "visible church" is not found in the Old or the New Testament. To discover the meaning of the concept requires some historical background.

God's original intent in Abraham was to call out a people that would bless the whole earth. It was also His intention that this people would be wholly dependent on Him. He would be their God, and they would be His people. God intended that He would be King.[1] God would speak to His people and lead them through His servants the prophets.

It wasn't long, however, until God's people wanted a king like the nations around them. This desire came to a head in the days of Samuel, the prophet, whose sons were evil persons. The people and the elders of Israel assembled. They said to Samuel, " 'Behold, you are old and your sons do not walk in your ways; now appoint for us a king to govern us like all the nations.' But the thing displeased Samuel when

---

1. See Genesis 12:1-3, Exodus 6:6, 7, and Judges 8:23. Gideon said, "I will not rule over you, and my son will not rule over you; the Lord will rule over you."

they said, 'Give us a king to govern us.' And Samuel prayed
to the Lord. And the Lord said to Samuel, 'Hearken to the
voice of the people in all that they say to you; for they have
not rejected you, but they have rejected me from being king
over them' '' (1 Samuel 8:5-7).

A king appeared among the people of God. Instead of
God's serving as King, a man became king, an arrangement
that was practiced in the nations around Israel. In retrospect,
the high point of Israel was not the time of King David. In
many ways this was a low point! For man tried to be king
instead of God. Though kings "ruled" Israel, yet God
continued to speak and to lead through the prophets. The
prophets were constantly prodding and correcting the kings.
In fact, to understand God's working with Israel, it is
necessary to see the kings through the eyes of the prophets.

The prophets kept working with the kings, pushing them
to rule the people of God as God intended. But the story is a
sad one. The kings refused to listen. The prophets' lives were
in peril.. Then Isaiah revealed an important insight. He
foretold a group of faithful people—"a remnant." Coming
out of the masses, yet in the midst of the masses would
emerge a group of faithful people. (See Isaiah 10:20-22,
11:11, 16.) This was a forerunner of the idea of a visible
church.

Pentecost was an unusual intervention of God. As noted in
the last chapter, a fundamental meaning of Pentecost, the
giving of the Holy Spirit, was God's calling out a special
people. To be a part of this people was in no way connected
with one's racial or cultural backgrounds. From many countries and languages, people heard the message in their own
tongues. Babel was reversed. In the making of a new people
was the call to repent and thus, "Save yourself from this
crooked generation!"

At Pentecost the new people met together. They fellow-shiped together. They ate together. They broke bread. They continued in the fellowship of the apostles. And this fellow-ship expanded throughout the known world.

But it was not long until the old ways of Israel cropped up in the church. Around AD 300 the church and state were brought together, this time under Constantine. Constantine was a politician. It has been said that he was not a troubled soul, but a troubled politician. Constantine was on the way to world conquest when he had a vision of the cross in the sky. In the legendary story, a voice said, "Conquer in this sign." Constantine saw Christianity as the means to pull off his plan for dominating the world.

Church and government were united in a way similar to Israel's when the people asked for a king. In retrospect, Constantine was the fall of the church, not the glory of the church! From Constantine's time, church and state went hand in hand. In the beginning, the church was oppressed by the state. But after Constantine, the state used its power to oppress those who were not Christians.

Theologians in Constantine's day (and since) have tried to justify this union in which the church is used for the benefit of the government. As church and state went hand in hand, New Testament views and understandings of the church were not being experienced. The tension was between the church as the body of Christ *(Corpus Christi)* and the church as all of society *(Corpus Christianum)*. In the former view, the church is a group of people called out of society. In the latter, everybody in society is Christian.

Later, Augustine, the great theologian, realized that "Corpus Christianum" in which everyone is a Christian (baptizing pagans by walking them through a stream) was not the church the New Testament knew. Then it occurred to him that within the masses of "Christians" there was a little church of the faithful. But no one knew who or where they were. They formed an "invisible church." Christendom was the visible church, in the midst of which was an invisible church.

Coupled with this, Augustine developed the notion of predestination. In this, no one really knows who will be in the church, since it is a matter of God's election. (Such ideas are still around today.)

In Augustine's time there was a group of believers called the Donatists. For them the church was a small body of the saved, visibly called out of the crooked generation, as envisioned at Pentecost. They saw that a church that embraced the whole citizenry was not the church of Jesus Christ.

Most of the Reformers, as did Augustine, said that in society (Christendom) there is a true church, but it is invisible. However, those within the believing church said the opposite. For them the church was visible, not because it embraced all people, but because it could be identified by the quality of the lives of those who are in it.

Augustine made interesting interpretations of Scripture to defend the church as made up of the masses. When the emperor compelled people to become Christians, Augustine justified this with a parable in Luke 14, where servants compelled people to come to a wedding feast. In the same way, Augustine said, the state could compel people to come into the church. He interpreted Daniel 3 (after Shadrach, Meshach, and Abednego were rescued, Nebuchadnezzar made an edict that the whole empire should not speak against their God) to be predictive prophecy, looking to the time when the emperor would do as Nebuchadnezzar had done. The emperor would make edicts to keep anyone from speaking against Christianity.

When the church was united with the state, the concept of nonresistance and defenselessness fell by the way. Luke 22:38 became an important text. The disciples said, "Look, Lord, here are two swords." Jesus replied, "It is enough." This became the basis for a doctrine of "two swords," the sword of the clergy and the sword of the government under one Head, Jesus Christ, to force everyone to become Christians. Thus personal decision to follow Jesus Christ was removed.

The need for repentance was gone. The idea of renewal of life was lost. The sense of mission in winning others was gone. Instead coercion was used.

Then the idea of sacraments came on the scene. Instead of baptism serving as a sign of entry into the body of Christ, it became a means whereby original sin was washed away. Since sin should be removed as soon as possible, infants were baptized. A person became a citizen of the state and a member of the church at the same time—at baptism.

The concept of grace was lost. Salvation came by being baptized and by participating in the Lord's Supper, which became the "mass." Salvation became a matter of pardon, not of repentance and renewal.

Church leaders became immoral. A view emerged that the quality of the life of a leader makes little difference. When the leader functions in a churchly capacity with the proper credentials, this is what is important.

All through history there have been those like the Donatists who have said "No" to these views. There were the followers of Huss. There were the Bohemian Brethren. There were the Waldensians. At the time of the Reformation, there were the Anabaptists. For them the church was a called-out group, a holy people, visible because of the quality of life lived as followers of Jesus Christ. The

Anabaptists saw the church as the body of Christ, not as invisible, lost in the masses, but as a group of holy brethren and sisters, highly visible because of their life of love and holiness.

The Anabaptist definition of the church and the definition put forth by the Reformers, such as Calvin or Luther, form a real watershed. The Anabaptists viewed the church as a "fellowship of saints, namely of all believing and regenerated Christians, children of God born again from above, by the word and the Spirit."[2] Over against this was Calvin's view of the church as "that mass of men among whom the word of God is purely preached and the sacraments administered according to the institution of Christ."[3]

Both Luther and Zwingli embraced the Christendom idea of the church. They talked about an invisible church in the midst of a Christian society. But this was contrary to the kind of church born at Pentecost—a faithful, visible group, following Jesus. The true church is not tucked away in Christendom, so that no one knows where it is nor who is involved. Rather, the true church is visible. Persons enter the church voluntarily. They decide; they repent; they receive new life. They are part of the body of Christ.

The usual concept of the church today is in large measure a product of what has gone before. Much that is heard today, whether from radio and television preachers or in popular religious magazines, reflects a Corpus Christianum perspective. The idea of a visible church is a fundamental concept of Anabaptist/Mennonite theology.

Only a disciplined church, however, is a visible church.

---

2. Leonard Verduin *The Anatomy of a Hybrid* (Grand Rapids, Mich.: Eerdmans, 1976), p. 201.

3. *Ibid.*

Without discipline, the church becomes like the world. In Matthew 16 Jesus asked His disciples, "But who do you say that I am?" Simon Peter replied, "You are the Christ, the Son of the living God."

Then Jesus said,

> "Blessed are you, Simon Bar-Jona! For flesh and blood has not revealed this to you, but my Father who is in heaven. And I tell you, you are Peter, and on this rock I will build my church, and the powers of death shall not prevail against it. I will give you the keys of the kingdom of heaven, and whatever you bind on earth shall be bound in heaven, and whatever you loose on earth shall be loosed in heaven" (Matthew 16:13-19).

In Matthew 18 Jesus said,

> "If your brother sins against you, go and tell him his fault, between you and him alone. If he listens to you, you have gained your brother. But if he does not listen, take one or two others along with you, that every word may be confirmed by the evidence of two or three witnesses. If he refuses to listen to them, tell it to the church; and if he refuses to listen even to the church, let him be to you as a Gentile and a tax collector. Truly, I say to you, whatever you bind on earth shall be bound in heaven, and whatever you loose on earth shall be loosed in heaven. Again I say to you, if two of you agree on earth about anything they ask, it will be done for them by my Father in heaven. For where two or three are gathered in my name, there am I in the midst of them" (Matthew 18:15-20).

The Greek word for church, *ekklesia,* appears in Matthew 16 and 18. It means "a called-out group." Notice that when the word "church" is on the lips of Jesus, it is in the context of binding and loosing! It should be observed in Matthew 16 that the confession "Jesus is the Messiah" or "Jesus is Lord" is basic to the church. A second characteristic should also be observed. The church is where believers are empowered to speak to one another concerning the will and the way of the Lord—to bind and loose.

In recent times it has been suggested that evangelism is the essence of the church. Statements, such as, "The church exists for mission as fire exists for burning," are heard. This is a good insight. But when Jesus spoke about the church, He did not stress evangelism. That came later in the Great Commission. Rather, Jesus stressed the central affirmation (Jesus is the Christ or Messiah), along with the nature of the community, where believers are binding and loosing.

A problem in the English language is that "you" is both singular and plural. Today "you" is often interpreted as singular, when in the original Greek it is plural. "You," plural, suggests a body. In Matthew 18 "you" is both singular and plural. If your brother (singular) sins against you,[4] go and tell him his fault between you (singular) and him alone. If he listens to you (singular), you (singular) have gained your brother. But if he does not listen, take one or two others along with you (singular) that every word may be confirmed by the evidence of two or three witnesses.[5] If he refuses to listen to them, tell it to the church. If he refuses to listen even to the church, let him be to you (singular) as a Gentile and a tax collector. Truly I say to you (plural), whatever you (plural) bind on earth shall be bound in heaven, and whatever you (plural) loose on earth shall be loosed in heaven. Again I say to you (plural), if two of you agree on

---

4. In some of the best Greek texts "against you" is not found. There is a strong possibility that this is a later addition. In some versions "against you" is deleted. This makes a much more powerful statement, "if your brother sins"—not just "against you"!

5. This is an important point. See Deuteronomy 19 and 15, where there is need for witnesses. This is repeated again in 2 Corinthians 13:1; 1 Timothy 5:19; and Hebrews 10:28.

earth about anything they ask, it will be done for them by my Father in heaven. For where two or three are gathered in my name, there am I in the midst of them.[6]

To bind has two meanings: (1) to withhold fellowship and (2) to forbid something or to make it obligatory.

To loose also has two meanings: (1) to forgive and (2) to free or permit.

Whenever Jesus said that He would forgive sins, this made trouble. People couldn't believe that a man could forgive sins. Yet this was what Jesus told His followers to do. See also John 20:21, where Jesus said, "If you forgive the sins of any, they are forgiven; if you retain the sins of any, they are retained." There are places in the New Testament that suggest that the Holy Spirit empowers for the witness. In John 20:21 the Holy Spirit is given for binding and loosing, and for forgiving!

People were scandalized when Jesus claimed to forgive sins. It was also scandalous when He told a group of tax collectors and fishermen to do something that only rabbis were allowed to do. The rabbis were to apply the law to cases brought to them.

Jesus' instructions to forgive are hard for Christians today. Because of abuses in the Roman Church before the Reformation and since, many believers have said that only God can forgive sin, that forgiveness of sin is merely assurance in one's heart, and that it is not mediated by men. Yet from the words of Jesus it is clear that believers are to mediate forgiveness to one another.

"If your brother sins . . ." (Matthew 18:15) assumes that

---

6. This statement has often been used as a rationale for poorly attended prayer meetings. It should, rather, be seen as a basic statement about the importance of the body being together to pray and to make decisions.

sin is identifiable. If not, how would persons know what sin is? Today, Christians seem able to identify when a person is saved, but unable to identify when a person is faithful! How many times is it said, "So and so was gloriously saved"? It's good when a person is "gloriously saved." But why is it Christians can't take the next step and discern when a person is "gloriously faithful"? Or when a person is "perilously unfaithful"?

"If your brother sins" suggests standards that are both knowable and known. These require prior discernment. Of course, that's why the Scriptures were given. All of life must come under the review and the judgment of the New Testament. If your brother sins, go and tell him his fault. Galatians 6 adds that this is to be done in the spirit of meekness.

Notice that neither Jesus nor the New Testament encourages impersonal applications of rules! John H. Yoder has observed that binding and loosing gives more authority to the church than does Rome. It trusts more to the Holy Spirit than does Pentecostalism. It has more respect for the individual than humanism. It makes moral standards more binding than Puritanism. It is more open to a given situation than the "new morality." If practiced it would change the life of churches more fundamentally than has yet been suggested by current, popular discussions of changing church structures.[7]

By going to a brother, his perspectives are discovered. In careful discussion and interaction a standard is altered, or reconfirmed, or together believers come to a new insight. When going to a brother, the situation is taken into account. Why did he behave as he did? In the discussion the reasons

---

7. John Howard Yoder, "Binding and Loosing," *Concern # 14*, February 1967, p. 12.

for the behavior may become clear. The need for changes are discerned. The church has stressed the power of the Holy Spirit to witness and to live a holy life, but John's Gospel makes it clear that the Holy Spirit also gives power to discern and to forgive.

Congregational discipline is of great importance. Without discipline the church loses its meaning. Without a meaningful church, evangelism loses its meaning. An ever more aggressive evangelism cannot make up for the neglect of discipline. Bigger and better crusades do not solve the problem of sin in the church. The call of evangelism not backed up by discipleship becomes cheap grace.

The essence of evangelism will be clarified when people see that conversion leads to a disciplined life in the church. Outreach will be benefited by a faithful, disciplined church.

There is fear that discipline leads to legalism. It does, if it is not grounded in the gospel. But laxity, or letting anything go, is not the answer to legalism. The gospel releases from sin—whether legalism or indulgence. Furthermore, discipline must be carried out redemptively and lovingly, not punitively. Discipline is an effort to reclaim persons from sin. As such it is not an embarrassment nor a disgrace.

Blunders of the past should not interfere with Jesus' command to bind and loose. The gospel is the good news that the sinner can be converted. It is also the good news that persons can live holy, Christlike lives. The church cannot accept the task of evangelism and then neglect discipline. Evangelism is undermined when people discover that in the absence of discipline to be a part of the church really makes little difference. Evangelism then becomes a religous experience for its own sake.

Much of modern evangelism fails to take seriously this basic part of the gospel—calling people into the church—

the visible community that accepts the rule of God and is already experiencing a foretaste of what will be in God's kingdom!

Ronald J. Sider writes, concerning binding and loosing, "I must confess that this topic scares me. Legalism, preoccupation with externals, concern for the letter rather than the spirit of biblical commands, authoritarian disregard for the individual freedom—these have so often been a part of church discipline in the past. It would be a ghastly tragedy if we would proceed to write still another sad chapter in the history of religious legalism and pious authoritarianism."

But, then he adds, "We don't give up on marriage just because so many people make a mess of it. Nor can we abandon the clear biblical call for church discipline just because it has so often been done so badly."[8]

The church must recapture this part of its faith heritage today. It must make reconciliation its goal. It must make gentle love, nurtured by prayer and tears, its means. And the Holy Spirit will use binding and loosing as one of His tools to help believers watch over each other in love, so that the church is indeed visible, a light in a dark world.

---

8. Ronald J. Sider, "Spare the Rod and Spoil the Church," *Eternity*, October 1976, p. 53.

The Community of the Spirit

In this chapter and next, the focus is on the church as the community of the Holy Spirit. In chapter 4 special attention is given to the Spirit's gifts and to His work of producing fruit in the lives of believers. In chapter 5 the focus shifts from inner life to the congregation's outward demonstration and witness in the world, as the Holy Spirit enables believers to act in love and to speak the words that free men.

In this chapter the gifts of the Spirit are examined and then some observations are made about them.

To begin, it may be helpful to review the charts. The first chart lists the gifts that are found in the four (or five) lists in the New Testament. (The chart uses the words found in the *New International Version.*)

(A) *1 Corinthians 12:8-10.* This passage lists nine gifts of the Spirit.

(B) *1 Corinthians 12:28.* This list suggests a priority—first, apostles; second, prophets; third, teachers. The other gifts are not given a precise ranking.

(C) *1 Corinthians 12:29, 30.* This list is in the form of a

CHART 1

A. 1 Corinthians 12:8-10, NIV
1. speak with wisdom
2. speak with knowledge
3. faith
4. gifts of healing
5. miraculous powers
6. prophecy
7. distinguish between spirits
8. speak in different kinds of tongues
9. interpretation of tongues

B. 1 Corinthians 12:28, NIV
1. apostles
2. prophets
3. teachers
4. workers of miracles
5. gifts of healing
6. able to help others
7. gifts of administration
8. speaking in different kinds of tongues

C. 1 Corinthians 12:29, 30, NIV
1. apostles
2. prophets
3. teachers
4. work miracles
5. gifts of healing
6. speak in tongues
7. interpret

D. Romans 12:6-8, NIV
1. prophesying
2. serving
3. teaching
4. encouraging
5. contributing (generously)
6. leadership (diligently)
7. showing mercy (cheerfully)

E. Ephesians 4:11, NIV
1. apostles
2. prophets
3. evangelists
4. pastors
5. teachers

F. Galatians 5:22-24, NIV Fruit of the Spirit—
1. love
2. joy
3. peace
4. patience
5. kindness
6. goodness
7. faithfulness
8. gentleness
9. self-control

Note parallels among:
1 Corinthians 13;
Romans 12:9-16;
Ephesians 4:12-16;
Galatians 5:26

series of questions. In the original language each of these questions is followed by a Greek particle which is not translated in the English versions. It means, "Surely not!" Thus, Are all apostles? *Surely not!* Are all prophets? *Surely not!* Are all evangelists? *Surely not!* Are all teachers? *Surely not!* Do all work miracles? *Surely not!* Do all have the gifts of healing? *Surely not!* Do all speak in tongues? *Surely not!* Do all interpret? *Surely not!*

(D) *Romans 12:6-8.* This passage lists seven gifts of the Spirit.

(E) *Ephesians 4:11.* Here "pastors-teachers" could be "pastors and teachers." In Ephesians gifts are seen as persons. In the other lists, the gifts are seen as abilities or skills.

(F) *Galatians 5:22-24.* These verses list nine qualities which together represent the Fruit of the Spirit in a Christian's life.

Chart 2 places the gifts in parallel columns. In this arrangement it becomes clear that only prophets and prophesying (or prophesy) appear in all the lists. Approximately 20 gifts are listed. But there are more. For example, in 1 Corinthians 7 Paul mentioned that he was without a wife. He wrote that he had the *gift* of celibacy which was given him by God. Thus celibacy could be added to the list of gifts.

Gifts are given for the good of the congregation. According to 1 Corinthians 12:7 gifts are given for the common good, for the good of the whole body. They are not given primarily for the benefit of the individual.

The gifts of *wisdom and knowledge.* Returning to Chart 1, it may be helpful to examine the gifts one by one. In 1 Corinthians 12:8, "speaking with wisdom" and "speaking with knowledge" are listed. Paul also refers to "wisdom" in 1

CHART 2

	1 Corinthians 12:8-10, NIV	1 Corinthians 12:28-31, NIV	Romans 12:6-8, NIV	Ephesians 4:11, NIV
1.	speak with wisdom			
2.	speak with knowledge			
3.	faith			
4.	gifts of healing	gifts of healing		
5.	miraculous power	workers of miracles		
6.	prophecy	prophets	prophesying	prophets
7.	distinguishing between spirits			
8.	speak in different kinds of tongues	speaking in different kinds of tongues		
9.	interpretation of tongues	interpret		
10.			serving	
11.		teachers	teaching	teachers
12.			encouraging	
13.			contributing	
14.			leadership	
15.			showing mercy	
16.		apostles		apostles
17.		gifts of administration		
18.				evangelists
19.				pastors
20.		able to help others		

dōrea—gift—of Holy Spirit—Acts 2:38; 8:20; 10:45; 11:17 (11 times in NT)
karisma—gifts of grace (17 times in NT)
pnūmatikos—"spiritual things"—1 Corinthians 12:1; 14:1 "spiritual (gifts)" (25 times in NT)

Corinthians 1:20-31, and in 1 Corinthians 8 he refers to "knowledge." Paul is opposed to the wisdom *of the world.* In the context of offering meat to idols, Paul writes that knowledge tends to puff up, whereas love builds up (1 Corinthians 8:1).

There are two kinds of wisdom and two kinds of knowledge. *Wisdom* and *knowledge* are not contrasted! Rather, human wisdom and human knowledge are contrasted with the wisdom and knowledge that come from God. The "word of wisdom" can be translated "the message of wisdom" or, as in the *New International Version,* "speak with wisdom" and "speak with knowledge." It is wrong to polarize wisdom and knowledge. Both are needed. If there is a polarization, it is between *human* wisdom and knowledge and *spiritual* wisdom and knowledge.

The message of wisdom given by the Holy Spirit is correct intuition or right insight. Knowledge implies research, investigation, and inquiry. The gift is the ability to present with effective reason the truth of the Christian faith.

It is important to realize that "heart" and "mind" are not contrasted. God made humans as unified beings. Both heart and mind are to be brought into conformity with Jesus Christ.

It is wrong to speak of Christian experience in terms of "head experience" or "heart experience." The point is that Christian experience requires both. The Spirit gives the message of wisdom and also the message of knowledge. Wisdom, according to the Greek preposition, is *through* the Spirit, and knowledge is in *accordance* with the Spirit. This suggests that God has made people so that the Holy Spirit can make use of their minds *and* their emotions! Both are to be used to His glory.

The gift of faith. This is not faith that saves. This faith is a gift. It leads to special, visible results. It involves an openness and confidence in God which enables the power of God to work through the person who has it.

The gifts of healing, or the gifts of cures. These gifts bring restoration to health. Incidentally, the healing gifts are plural. Paul suggests that the Holy Spirit enables Christians with these gifts to heal a variety of illnesses. These gifts may work miraculously. They may simply remove blocks to healing, or they may increase the speed of healing. Nevertheless, the gifts of healing are identifiable and demonstrate the presence and work of God in healing a variety of sicknesses.

The gift of miraculous power. In the original language the word power appears. "The operations of powers" is another way to translate this. This has a dual meaning. It refers to the ability to do miraculous things. God can and does perform miracles. It also suggests that persons are able to demonstrate extraordinary strength. This was characteristic of the Apostle Paul. He was able to travel across the face of the earth, to suffer and to endure persecution, yet he kept on going with unbelievable strength. This is another meaning of "the operation of powers."

The gift of prophecy. Prophecy also has two meanings: (1) prophecy predicts the future; and (2) prophecy makes clear here and now the will of God. In the New Testament, Agabus foretold famine (Acts 11:28). In the light of his prophecy, the church decided to plan a relief program. Another time Agabus took Paul's girdle and warned what would happen if Paul returned to Jerusalem (Acts 21:10). This was the predictive dimension. On a continuum of one to ten, it's not clear how much of prophecy involves prediction—possibly at 2 or 3 on the scale. The larger meaning of prophecy is to convey God's will to His church now. Prophecy is the divinely given ability to sense the will of God and to make it known to brothers and sisters. Prophecy also includes the convicting of conscience that leads people to action. On the same continuum surely this would be at 9 or 10.

The gift of distinguishing between spirits. Almost all of God's manifestations have satanic counterparts. This is true in the Book of Revelation with its heavenly world and the world below—angels of God and the angels from beneath, smoke in the heavenly temple and the smoke from the pit. There is the name for God and the name for Satan, which is just the opposite. Satan counterfeits the acts of God. Believers, therefore, must distinguish the true from the counterfeit. This is especially true of prophecy. Paul writes (1 Corinthians 14:29-33) that when a prophet speaks, the whole congregation should weigh what is said. Christians must also weigh the gifts that are being exercised. Are they of God? Of Satan? Or self-induced? The ability to distinguish between spirits, to discover who is guided by the Spirit and who is not, is an important gift.

The gifts of speaking in different kinds of tongues and of interpreting tongues. Is the gift of tongues the same as at Pentecost? There seem to be differences between the speaking at Pentecost and speaking with tongues described in 1 Corinthians 12, 13, and 14. At Pentecost when believers spoke, "Each one heard them speaking in his own language" (Acts 2:6). In 1 Corinthians 12, 13, and 14 an interpreter is needed. Interpretation is required so everyone can understand, and thus the gift can contribute to the common good.

Now a few comments about the rest of the twenty gifts in Chart 2. In Romans 12:7 the ministry of service is mentioned. This appears after prophecy and before teaching. It may refer to the work traditionally done by the deacon. In 1 Timothy 3:13, Paul wrote that "those who serve well as deacons gain a good standing for themselves and also great confidence in the faith which is Christ Jesus." The Greek word for "service" is the root for the word "deacon."

The next gift is teaching or teacher. The apostle was able to proclaim the will and way of God. The prophet could make clear the will of God. The teacher did the same. There is overlapping of function among apostles and prophets and teachers. Fundamentally, the teacher had the responsibility to make clear Christian doctrine—the truths of the gospel. The teacher also made clear the ethical implications of the gospel, by expounding the Word of God.

Exhorting goes with teaching like wisdom goes with knowledge. Teaching is directed to a person's mind and understanding, while exhortation is directed to a person's conscience and will. Exhortation is to help believers persevere in the faith and to be patient. Exhortation also includes consolation, especially of those who are in difficulty.

The list in Romans 12 also includes "contributing." The serving of the deacon implied making use of funds and resources of the congregation. Here contributing refers to private or individual funds. This gift involves the ability to share of one's possessions. Giving is to be done with simplicity—with a single-minded motive. The giver is not to give to secure influence, nor advantage, nor to secure one's own way. When a congregation or churchwide body makes a decision, some members may not like it. But as a brotherhood, members go along with each other. Christians don't refuse to give because they don't like the congregation's action.

Another gift is "taking the lead." This is similar to "governments" (1 Corinthians 12). It is the ability to exercise oversight. It involves being a shepherd, which is part of the task of a pastor.

Another gift is "showing mercy." This is to show directly and currently an interest in someone in need. Acts of mercy are to be done graciously. Often, Christians hesitate to enter into the problems of others. Often, too, entry into such problems is misunderstood. Sometimes helping others is a disagreeable task. Sometimes it turns out to be a thankless activity. Nevertheless, this gift enables believers to continue to show mercy.

An important work of the apostle was mission outreach. An apostle was a "sent one." A basic qualification was to have been an eyewitness of Jesus. Apostles were deeply involved in the expansion of the church. They pushed the edges of the church farther and farther into the world.

The gift of governing, like taking the lead, is the ability to administer. This gift should not be minimized. Good administration is important in the life of the church.

The gift of evangelists centers in persons who extend the church. Philip and others could be mentioned. The evangelist and the apostle had overlapping functions.

The gift of pastors or shepherds is a beautiful word picture. Such persons have the gift to feed the church, to guide the church, to protect the church.

The gift of "helps" is similar to ministry and service. This is a ministry of aid, and is likely best described in the work of the deacon.

The listing of gifts illustrates how extensive they are. At no point should the list be considered exhaustive. Nor is there an order of importance—first, second, and third. All gifts are necessary for the congregation to function effectively!

Now some observations.

1. *A variety of words are used to refer to gifts.* There is *dōrea.* This word is used in Acts for the gift of the Holy Spirit (Acts 2:38). The Holy Spirit Himself was given.

Another word is *karisma.* Sometimes this word is used for special gifts in general. Sometimes it is applied to gifts given to the whole group or congregation (Romans 12 and 1 Corinthians 12). At times this word refers to a gift given to an individual. This is the case in 1 Peter 4:10. Each one receives a gift.

A third is the word *pnūmatikos,* which can be translated "spiritual things." For some reason English translations use the word "gifts." "Now concerning spiritual things" probably would be a more accurate translation than "spiritual gifts." This word appears 25 times in the New Testament.

In the English language there is one word for gift. Fine distinctions are absent. Usually *dōrea* refers to the giving of the Spirit, while *karisma* refers to spiritual gifts.

2. *Gifts, though often called gifts of the Spirit, could as well be called "gifts of God."* In 1 Corinthians 12:4-6 the trinity appears: "Now there are varieties of gifts, but the same *Spirit,* and there are varieties of service, but the same *Lord,* and there are varieties of working, but it is the same *God* who inspires them all in every one." In 1 Corinthians 12:27 Paul wrote, "Now you are the body of Christ and individually members of it. And *God* has appointed in the church first apostles, second prophets, third teachers." In the list of gifts in Romans 12 the Holy Spirit is not mentioned at all. Of course, God works through the Holy Spirit. It is helpful not to limit the origin of gifts to the Holy Spirit.

Gifts are given as God chooses. God can give one or several gifts. No one person has all the gifts. Nor is one gift the possession of all believers! This is especially clear when Paul wrote, "Are all apostles? Certainly not! Are all prophets? Certainly not! Are all teachers? Certainly not! Do all work miracles? Certainly not! Do all possess gifts of healing? Certainly not! Do all speak with tongues? Certainly not! Do all interpret? Certainly not! But desire earnestly the higher gifts" (1 Corinthians 12:29-31). In 1 Corinthians 14:1 Paul writes, "Make love your aim, and earnestly desire the spiritual gifts, especially that you may *prophesy*." Prophecy is the one gift that appears in all the lists of gifts.

3. *Gifts are the* power *in the church, but over the years, and even now, they have created* problems *in the church.* Christians have allowed gifts to divide. They have allowed gifts to become a basis for fellowship. God intended that gifts, when exercised properly, would produce harmony.

It is in the context of the discussion of the gifts that Paul wrote most pointedly about love. In Romans 12, after listing gifts such as prophecy, service, teaching, and exaltation, contribution and giving aid, and acts of mercy, Paul wrote, "Let love be genuine.... Love one another with brotherly affection; outdo one another in showing honor" (vv. 9, 10). After listing gifts in 1 Corinthians 12, Paul followed with his major description of love. Notice, too, that 1 Corinthians 13 relates gifts to love: tongues (v. 1)—without love they are a noisy gong or a clanging symbol; prophetic powers, knowledge, faith (v. 2), liberal giving (v. 3)—without love are worthless. Prophecies pass away. Tongues cease. Knowledge passes away. Faith, hope, and love remain. The greatest of these is love!

After listing the gifts for equipping, Paul added (Ephesians 4) that Christians are to speak the truth in love, and everything is to grow and upbuild itself in love (vv. 15, 16). Whenever gifts are mentioned, it seems there follows a stress on love. Gifts, though they demonstrate power in the church, turn out to be a problem whenever they are exercised without love!

4. *Believers are not to test each other by the presence or*

absence of gifts. God gives gifts as He will. Believers are to test each other by the fruit of the Spirit. In the final analysis believers are to be conformed to the image of His Son (Romans 8:29). This is why the fruit of the Spirit—love, joy, peace, patience, kindness, goodness, faithfulness, gentleness, self-control—are so important. They are traits of Christlikeness.

The fundamental question that faces believers within the body of Christ is not "What gifts?" but rather, "How Christlike?"

CHAPTER 5

The Church Empowered by the Holy Spirit

The last chapter focused on gifts of the Spirit to the congregation. This chapter considers the work of the Holy Spirit in thrusting the congregation into the world to witness and to serve. Remember, a purpose of gifts is to equip saints for ministry in the world (Ephesians 4:12).

A striking thing in the New Testament is the constant appearance of the word "power." Often this is not visible in English translations because the Greek word *dunamis* is translated in many ways. Sometimes it is translated "power," sometimes "mighty works," sometimes "ability." When the woman touched the hem of Jesus' garment and was healed, Jesus perceived that "virtue had gone out of him" (KJV). This archaic translation from the 1600s simply meant that power had gone from Him. The word is also translated "miracle" and sometimes "strength." The word *dunamis* appears at least 120 times in the New Testament.

The story of the church and the message of the gospel are a story and message of *power!* Originally, the Greek word meant "to be able," "capacity," or "to be capable of." This

is but a short step to power and might. Thus when the Holy
Spirit empowers the church, the Spirit makes believers *able*.
He gives believers the *capacity* to do the will of God. Believers become *capable* of carrying out the tremendous task of
bringing a witness to the world.

It is important to maintain a trinitarian viewpoint. In the
New Testament power is not attributed only to the Holy
Spirit. Constantly, there is reference to the *power of God*
and to the *power of Jesus Christ*. Power is thus intertwined
in the Godhead. The power of God, the power of Jesus
Christ, and the power of the Holy Spirit must be kept in
perspective. There was the danger of cults in the Corinthian
church, for example, a Jesus cult. Today there tend to be
cults of the Holy Spirit. There are also cults which focus only
on God.

It may be helpful to review some of the New Testament
passages that deal with (1) the power of God, (2) the power
of Jesus Christ, and (3) the power of the Holy Spirit.

1. *The power of God*. When the Sadducees came to Jesus
with a tricky question about the resurrection, they told an
odd story about the death of a man who had been married
many times. They wondered, who would be married to
whom in heaven? To this Jesus replied, "You know neither
the scripture nor the *power* of God!" (Matthew 22:29; Mark
12:24). That was an appropriate answer to a tricky question!
In 1 Corinthians 1:18 Paul wrote about the cross—that it is
folly to the world, but to those who are being saved it is the
power of God.

In 1 Corinthians 1:24 Paul wrote that the gospel is
universal—calling both Jews and Greeks. Christ is the *power*
of God. Later Paul wrote about his ministry to the Corinthian church. He said that their faith was a response to His
teaching and to his life in their midst. It did not rest in the

wisdom of men, but in the *power of God.* .

Paul wrote about the Christian life (1 Corinthians 6:14), noting how God raised the Lord, and how He will also raise believers by His *power.*

In 2 Corinthians 6:3-10 Paul defended his apostleship. People were critical of him, and were following the "super apostles" of his day. Paul described his life in their midst, his sufferings, his message, and work of the Holy Spirit. Paul also added that he demonstrated the *power of God.*

In 2 Corinthians 13:4 Paul included a saying about Jesus:

He was crucified in weakness, but lives by the *power of God.*

Then Paul added:

For we are weak in him, but in dealing with you we shall live with him by the *power of God.*

Paul was aware that his ministry as an apostle was a gift of God's grace. He acknowledged that it was given him by the *power of God* (Ephesians 3:7). Clearly, the call to service is a gift, and the ability to act springs from the power of God.

2. *The power of Jesus Christ.* When Jesus called the Twelve and sent them out, He gave them power and authority over all demons and to cure diseases. Jesus gave them *all power* (Luke 9:1).

In 1 Corinthians 5 an interesting phrase about the power of Jesus appears. Paul wrote that it was necessary for the congregation to deal with a sinning brother who was unrepentant. He told the congregation to discipline that brother. He wrote, "When you are assembled, and my spirit is present [that is when your understanding of the gospel that has come from me is present], with the *power of our Lord Jesus,* you are to deliver this man to Satan" (1 Corinthians 5:4).

Peter wrote, "We have made known to you the *power* and the coming of our Lord Jesus Christ" (2 Peter 1:16). The name "Lord Jesus Christ" is a basic affirmation of the church. As Lord, Jesus is King; He has first place. The name "Jesus" testifies to the fact that He was indeed a man, Jesus of Nazareth. "Christ" means the "anointed one" or "Messiah." Thus the name "Lord Jesus Christ" is itself a great Christian confession. It is His power, Peter wrote, that is made known!

In 2 Corinthians Paul wrote about a thorn in the flesh. It is not clear what this was—perhaps a physical illness. Paul prayed to the Lord Jesus for its removal. The Lord responded to his request with these words, "My grace is sufficient for you, for my *power* is made perfect in weakness" (2 Corinthians 12:9). To the Philippians Paul wrote that he wanted to know the *power* of Jesus' resurrection (3:10).

3. *The power of the Holy Spirit*. Jesus, after His temptation in the wilderness, returned in the *power of the Spirit* into Galilee (Luke 4:14).

Many of Jesus' references to power referred to Pentecost. He said, "Behold, I send the promise of my Father upon you; but stay in the city, until you are clothed with *power* from on high [the power of the Holy Spirit]" (Luke 24:49).

In the first chapter of Acts Jesus said to His disciples, "You shall receive *power* when the Holy Spirit has come upon you; and you shall be my witnesses in Jerusalem and in all Judea and Samaria and to the end of the earth" (1:8).

Paul prayed for the church at Rome, "That by the *power of the Holy Spirit* you may abound in hope" (Romans 15:13). He concluded his epistle to Rome, "For I will not venture to speak of anything except what Christ has wrought through me to win obedience from the Gentiles, by word and deed, by the *power* of signs and wonders, by the *power of the Holy Spirit,* so that from Jerusalem and as far round as Illyricum I have fully preached the gospel of Christ" (15:18, 19).

Paul attributed his effectiveness in witnessing and preaching to the power of the Holy Spirit. He wrote to the Corinthians, "My speech and message were not in plausible words of wisdom, but in demonstration of the Spirit and of *power*" (1 Corinthians 2:4). Paul wrote to the Thessalonians, "Our gospel came to you not only in word, but also in *power* and in the Holy Spirit and with full conviction" (1 Thessalonians 1:5).

In references to the power of the Holy Spirit, one thing stands out. In almost every instance the power of the Holy Spirit is manifested in the outward thrust of the church! Jesus said to wait for power for witnessing. The Book of Acts tells how the Holy Spirit was a driving force to send out the church. Paul attributed his effectiveness as an apostle to the power of the Holy Spirit! Thus to speak of the church empowered by the Holy Spirit is to stress the outreach or expansion of the church.

Another word should be said about Pentecost. One of the marvels of Pentecost was speaking in tongues. Persons from different countries and with different dialects were able to understand the event and its meaning in their own language. This was different from the speaking in tongues described in 1 Corinthians 14, where one who spoke in tongues needed another with the gift of interpretation for the good of the congregation.

The tongues of Pentecost made clear that Babel (where persons tried to climb to heaven and enter the presence of God by their own efforts) had been reversed. Now God had come in His Son, Jesus Christ. And in the giving of the Holy Spirit, the separation of people symbolized by the confusion of languages at Babel, was overcome.

Further, Pentecost was the fulfillment of Jesus' promise to give the Holy Spirit. Jesus said, "I came to cast fire upon the earth; and would that it were already kindled!" (Luke 12:49). John the Baptist said that he came baptizing with water, but there is one coming who will baptize with the Holy Spirit and with fire (Luke 3:16). At Pentecost there were tongues of fire!

Pentecost was the inauguration by the Holy Spirit of a new age, a new covenant, a new people! The coming of the Holy Spirit also inaugurated a new mission, to call persons into a new community. As Peter said at Pentecost, "It shall be that whoever calls on the name of the Lord shall be saved" (Acts 2:21).

Pentecost was followed by a series of mini-Pentecosts as the church entered new frontiers. Every time the church came to a new barrier on the frontier, a remarkable demonstration of the Holy Spirit's power occurred.

The first of the mini-Pentecosts was with the Samaritans. The question was, "Is it possible that Samaritans can receive the gospel?" The Jews hated the Samaritans and looked on them as outcasts. (It was remarkable that earlier Jesus took time to talk to a Samaritan woman. See John 4.) So the church sent Peter and John to investigate. They saw that the Christian experience of the Samaritans was real. Then apostles laid their hands on the Samaritans, and they received the Holy Spirit! (Acts 8:14).

A second manifestation of the Spirit's power was Paul's conversion on the Damascus road. Sometimes his conversion is described as instantaneous. It is probably more correct to think of it as a longer process. At least three days were involved. On the Damascus road, Paul was blinded. He was taken into the city unable to walk, and was left there alone.

It was difficult for the Spirit to lead some of the brothers to meet this persecutor of the church. But after three days Ananias came and laid his hands on Paul. Paul received his sight and was filled with the Holy Spirit. Then he was baptized.

Ananias laid his hands on Paul. Jesus also put His hands on persons to heal them. To "put on hands" was to commit a person to service. There is much symbolism in Paul's conversion experience. The three days of blindness in some respects resembled the three days Jesus was in the tomb. When Paul received his sight, the light spoke of resurrection. In any case, Ananias came to Paul, placed his hands on him, and his sight was restored. Paul was filled with the Holy Spirit and was baptized. Certainly, turning Paul "from persecutor to apostle" was a tremendous manifestation of the Holy Spirit's power. Paul, more than anyone else, was responsible for taking the gospel to the ends of the earth.

A third crisis arose in the church. Peter was involved in a controversy because he had taken the gospel to Cornelius, a Gentile. The gospel leaped from the Jewish family to their religious next of kin—the Samaritans—and now it reached the Gentiles. When Peter and Cornelius shared the meaning of the gospel, the Holy Spirit fell on all who heard.

Peter was amazed that the Holy Spirit had been poured out on Gentiles. People were speaking in other tongues and praising God. Then they were baptized.

Peter got into trouble when he reported to the church that the Gentiles were brought into the kingdom. But Peter responded to his critics, "I remembered the word of the Lord, how he said, 'John baptized with water, but you shall be baptized with the Holy Spirit.' If then God gave the same gift to them that he gave to us when we believe in the Lord Jesus Christ, who was I that I could withstand God?" (Acts

11:16). The Holy Spirit pushed out the church and broke down barriers.

The fourth mini-Pentecost was at Ephesus, with a group of persons who knew only the baptism of John. It would be good to know more about these people. Not all those who followed John the Baptist, and were baptized by him, became followers of Jesus. In fact, some of John's followers maintained their identity and opposed the followers of Jesus. Perhaps this explains why the writer of John's Gospel repeatedly emphasized that Jesus was superior to John the Baptist. He did this in the prologue, stating that John was not that light, but was sent to bear witness to that light. Later, he quoted John the Baptist, who said, "He must increase, I must decrease!"

It seems clear that some friction continued between the two groups. In Acts 19 followers of John the Baptist come in contact with the gospel of Jesus Christ as it was preached in the *power of the Holy Spirit.* The followers of John were asked, "Did you receive the Holy Spirit when you believed?" They replied, "No, we have never heard that there is a Holy Spirit." They were asked, "Into what then were you baptized?" The group replied, "Into John's baptism." Then Paul explained, "John baptized with a baptism of repentance, telling the people to believe in the one who was to come after him, that is, Jesus." On hearing this, John's followers were baptized in the name of the Lord Jesus. When Paul laid his hands upon them, the Holy Spirit was poured out. They spoke with tongues and prophesied.

This was an interesting sequence. Here were New Testament "Anabaptists"—they were rebaptized! This is the only incident of rebaptism in the New Testament. When John's disciples were rebaptized in the name of Jesus, the power of the Holy Spirit came upon them.

The Holy Spirit thrust the church from Jerusalem and Judea to Samaria, and then to the uttermost parts of the earth. The Holy Spirit forced the church to leap man-made barriers. The Holy Spirit fell on the Samaritans, then on the Gentiles, and even on a group of followers of John the Baptist who may have been causing difficulty for the followers of Jesus.

The Holy Spirit thrust the church into the world to proclaim the gospel of Jesus Christ. The evangelism of Acts and the epistles, however, seems different from the evangelism of today. Then evangelism was not reduced to verbal communication or techniques.

Much evangelism today seems too shallow and too oral. It's as though evangelism can somehow be reduced to repeating several key statements, or to accepting an easy plan. However, at Pentecost when the fire fell, Peter called the people to *repent!* He called them to save themselves from (or "to leave") the crooked generation! He called people to enter into and to participate in the new people of God!

Research has been done on some of the more modern ways of doing evangelism. An evangelistic campaign in a Midwestern city claimed a large number of conversions— people who made some response to the message of the evangelist. However, the researchers discovered that only a small proportion of these participated in any kind of Bible study following the campaign, and only a few persons actually became members of a congregation.

In evangelism it is important to observe this sequence of events: first *demonstration,* then *explanation,* and finally, *declaration!* At Pentecost this was beautifully seen. There was a demonstration of power. Peter explained what happened. Then he declared who Jesus was. The order seems to be reversed today, where the movement is from verbal to nonverbal. In the early church the movement was from non-verbal (the quality of the life of the community) to verbal.

It is no accident that Jesus referred to the community of faith as a city. He said that, like a city set on a hill, it cannot be hidden (Matthew 5:14). This is contrary to today's thinking. For many the city is the center of iniquity, the unsafe, blacktop jungle. This was not the way the city was seen in Jesus' day. Then the city was the center of civilized life. Un-civilized behavior and danger lay largely outside the city. Robbers threatened travelers along the road to Jericho, not in Jericho. The city enjoyed political order. The city was the center of commerce. The city represented abundance and security. The walls kept out invaders, providing safety. This was Jesus' view of the city. No wonder He used the city as a symbol of the community of faith.

As the city was the center of civilized life, so the church is the center of new life in Christ. As the city was the center of political order, so the church is the center of a new order that springs from love, concern, and compassion. As the city was the center of commerce and abundance, so now "the city that is set on a hill" is noted for its sharing and concern one for another. And when it comes to security, in this city God dwells in power.

Evangelism cannot be reduced to a series of words. This is the weakness of electronic evangelism. As good and im-portant as this witness may be, when electronic signals are sent out, no disciple nor community of faith is present for the viewer or listener to relate to. They do not follow the biblical order of demonstration, then explanation, and fi-nally declaration! The authority for the truth of the gospel is not tied ultimately to a declaration about an "infallible" Bi-ble. The authority and truth of the gospel are tied to the life, vitality, and reality of the disciples' faith and the reality of the community in which Jesus Christ dwells.

Here is where tribute should be paid to charismatic brethren and sisters. They are not satisfied merely with words! They are concerned that the gospel reveals power and demonstrates power in the lives of people. The power to which they bear witness goes beyond talk and logic.

Finally, there has also been a tendency over the centuries for Christians to divide Christian experience into stages. This was true among the infant baptizers. If a baby was baptized, at some point along the way it was felt that a second rite was necessary—confirmation. The puritans also did this. They spoke about conversion on one hand, and then about "confirmation of sonship" or assurance. They called the second stage the baptism of the Spirit.

The Wesleyans did a similar thing. They talked about an initial experience of conversion and a second experience of sanctification which they called the baptism of the Spirit. The line from a hymn, "Be of sin the double cure, save from wrath, and make me pure," reflects this twofold Wesleyan view of the working of the Spirit.°

Pentecostalism has also emphasized conversion, followed by a Pentecostal experience that involves speaking in tongues.

From the Book of Acts, it is difficult to make any sequence a norm. There were those who heard the gospel, the Holy Spirit came, and they were baptized. In the case of Paul, whatever happened extended over a three-day period. Paul did not write about his own experience as though it were in stages.

The New Testament speaks of coming to faith in Jesus

°A. M. Toplady, "Rock of Ages! Cleft for Me," stanza 1.

Christ, becoming a part of the body of Jesus, and receiving the Holy Spirit without emphasis on sequence. For by one Spirit we were all baptized into one body—Jews or Greeks, slaves or free—and all were made to drink of one Spirit (1 Corinthians 12:13). Further, Paul wrote of "*one* Lord, *one* faith, *one* baptism" (Ephesians 4:5).

Clearly, the Holy Spirit is the driving force in the expansion of the church. The Spirit is active. The New Testament speaks of many ways in which the Spirit works: the Spirit indwells; the Spirit knows (He knows the mind of God, as well as the inner mind of believers); the Spirit intercedes; the Spirit loves; the Spirit gives gifts; the Spirit leads; the Spirit convicts; the Spirit guides a new people!

At Pentecost the Holy Spirit created a new people, the church. As in Acts, so today the Holy Spirit thrusts Christians into new frontiers, and gives them the ability or capacity to do the Lord's will. At the same time He prepares those who will receive the witness. The Holy Spirit gives new life, and He adds to the church.

CHAPTER 6

The Wholeness of Salvation

This chapter focuses on salvation. A lot of what is done in the name of Christ is scandalous. In an announcement for revival meetings a newspaper ad gave these credentials for the evangelist: He was a former football coach and a Marine officer in Vietnam. He was critically wounded in combat, had undergone 22 operations, and had received the bronze and silver stars as well as three purple hearts. He had appeared on the Billy Graham and Jerry Falwell programs. Obviously, some dialogue is needed. In the understanding of the gospel presented in this book, it is difficult to be a witness for the Prince of Peace if one's main credentials are those listed above!

This study did not begin with salvation. It began with Jesus and His church, because the church offers salvation. When persons come to Jesus Christ, they become a part of His body, the church. The church is the context for thinking about salvation.

In an earlier chapter it was noted that where persons begin in interpreting the Bible influences their conclusions.

To emphasize the need to love the Bible and to believe the Bible is scarcely enough. To emphasize the need to believe certain things about the inspiration of the Bible is not enough since a doctrine of inspiration gives little assistance in interpretation. In fact, some of the poorest interpretations of the Bible are defended on the basis of an inerrant Bible!

In the days of the New Testament, people were living in a Greek-thinking world. Further, the thought patterns of our 20th-century society do not have their roots in Judaism. North American thinking is also rooted in the Greek world. The biblical understandings of the words "saved" and "salvation" have been skewed as Greek understandings have been read into both the New Testament and Old Testament words for these concepts.

The Greek world was filled with many gods. These gods did not have personal relationships with people. This is a significant difference from the Hebrew and Christian way of thinking, where God is very personal. He relates directly to people, and is not a Being to speculate about only in intellectual terms. I remember an Old Testament scholar saying that in the Greek world persons would talk about a god who is omnipotent (all powerful), omniscient (knows everything), or omnipresent (is everywhere). These abstract views of the Christian God are not wrong. But the Bible does not think about God in this way. The scholar said that if you asked a person in the Hebrew tradition what God is like he would reply, "God is like this: We were in captivity in Egypt and with His strong arm He led us out!" This is a personal God, a God deeply involved in the lives of His people.

The Greeks thought the gods might capriciously save an individual from danger. A god was like a king who could save a person or put him to death. He could keep people alive or kill them, accountable to no one. A god might give a benefit once in a while; he might provide a cure or keep one in good health. But their gods were capricious and nonpersonal. In the Hebrew way of thinking, salvation meant "to be roomy," the opposite of being "hemmed in," or "oppressed." To be saved is to be opened to new freedom, to new horizons—to move into an open place.

God saves, of course, through persons. There was a Moses, and a Gideon, and a David. It is equally clear, however, that the person himself didn't do it. God was at work. Human ability was limited. God acted and, ultimately, as the Old Testament bore witness, the deliverance was God's.

The prophets stressed that idols could not help (Isaiah 45:20; 46:7). Astrologers could not help (47:13). Angels could not help. Isaiah made the point that those who wait on the Lord renew their strength (40:31). God is a shepherd who leads His people out of captivity (Ezekiel 34:22; 36:24-29).

In the New Testament the Old Testament view of salvation is modified by Jesus. It's striking to see what Matthew and Luke wrote about "saved" and "salvation." Zechariah, at the birth of John the Baptist (Luke 1:73, 77), spoke of Israel's being saved from enemies, and that God will forgive sins. The name of Jesus meant "he will save his people from their sins" (Matthew 1:21). The New Testament, as well as the Old Testament, looks at salvation from a community rather than on an individual basis. That cuts across much of today's thinking. Jesus saves *His people* from their sins. Lonely Greek individualism is not here! Simeon spoke of "thy salvation" which is light to the Gentiles and a glory to Israel. Mary, when she received the promise of a Son, spoke of a tremendous upheaval in society. She saw in Jesus' salvation the scattering of the proud, putting down the mighty, exalting the lowly, filling the hungry, and turning the rich away empty (Luke 1:46-55). Thus salvation was not only an individual matter.

These are striking views of "saved" and "salvation." A study of salvation from a biblical basis and an Anabaptist perspective will break the narrowly confined views typical of current evangelical Christianity.

This is an era when the catch phrase, "born again," is popular. It appears everywhere, and truly it is an important concept. Jesus said to Nicodemus, "You must be born anew." The figure of new birth appears a number of times—in 1 Peter and in 1 John. It is a description of something that happens in salvation, in conversion. However, salvation cannot be limited to this one symbol of new birth. Jesus also said to the woman at the well that she should *drink the living water* (John 4:14). Jesus said to the crowd that He fed, that they should *eat the bread that came down from heaven* (John 6:48-52). Jesus said to the crowd at the feast (John 8:12) that they are to *have the light of life.* Constantly, Jesus used the most important phrase of all, *"Follow Me"* (John 1:43; 12:26; 21:19, 22). The firm admonition to follow Jesus underscores the tremendous importance of knowing His life and His teaching.

On a continuum of one to ten, if "born again" were at seven in importance, "Follow Me" would be at least eight or nine! Jesus also spoke of taking up the cross and following Him. Following Jesus is at the heart of making Him central. Jesus also used the words "saved" and "salvation." To Zacchaeus, Jesus said, "Today salvation has come to this house, since he also is a son of Abraham. For the Son of man came to seek and to save the lost" (Luke 19:9, 10). These words got Jesus into trouble. Not only was He fellowshiping with those excluded from the religious society—the tax collectors, prostitutes, and other outcasts—He was rescuing or saving

them. The self-righteous were critical because Jesus sought
such persons. The Greek word *sōzo*—"to save"—is also
translated "to make whole" or "to make well."

When Jesus healed blind Bartimaeus, He said, "Your
faith has made you well." This is the same word Jesus used
with the woman at Simon's house, when He said, "Your
faith has saved you" (Luke 7:50). Salvation is not limited to
the soul. Salvation involves the whole person.

For Paul salvation was the goal of his missionary
endeavors. He was concerned that all Jews be saved
(Romans 10:1). He wrote, "I try to please all men in everything I do, not seeking my own advantage, but that of many,
that they may be saved" (1 Corinthians 10:33). "I have become all things to all men, that I might by all means save
some" (1 Corinthians 9:22). Paul was concerned about those
who were hindering Him and His helpers from speaking to
Gentiles that they be saved (1 Thessalonians 2:16).

Now a few observations:

1. *Salvation dare not be reduced to accepting a series of
propositions.* Today there is a tendency to reduce salvation
to a set of beliefs, which when accepted intellectually is said
to lead to salvation. This fits into a theology which begins
with the writings of Paul rather than with the Gospels. This
is where Luther began—he stressed that one is saved by
faith only. Luther found his experience in Romans 1:16, thus
he constantly reiterated that salvation is by faith and not of
works. Unfortunately faith was reduced to belief, works to
legalism. The result of this has been to take salvation away
from life and make it an intellectual exercise. Many
preachers say something to this effect, "If you believe this,
and this, and this, then on the authority of God's Word, I
can say that you are saved."

This view of salvation is in harmony with the view of the

church as "the masses among whom the gospel is preached and the sacraments are properly observed." It also feeds notions of an invisible church. This is in contrast with the view of the church as a community of believers, who have been born again, who have drunk of the living water, who are a fellowship of the Spirit, who are binding and loosing. Here salvation involves participation in a community, where brothers and sisters *follow Jesus!*

2. *Salvation involves the whole person.* The concept of "saving souls" is not found in the Scripture—as though the target of evangelism were "souls." The Greek word *psukee* is translated in the King James Version as "soul." More often it is translated "life." This is a better translation. Here again Greek views have crept in. The Greeks viewed man as soul and body. For them the soul was good, the body was evil. The body was a prison house for the soul. It was necessary, therefore, to help release the soul from the body. This was foreign to Hebrew views. For them the body was created by God, and was good! The soul (which is also mentioned) was related to life. It involved the total personality. Just as there is nothing like an "invisible church," so there is nothing like an "invisible Christian." In the same way it is hard to think of a soul apart from a body. In fact, the Hebrew view was just opposite of the Greek view. The Greeks looked forward to death and the release of the immortal soul. The Hebrew hope, however, was for the resurrection of the body!

The self is a unity. Inner-experience and inner-awareness lead to outward behavior. They cannot be separated. Paul made the point that we must all appear before the judgment seat of Christ, so that each one may receive good or evil, according to what he has *done in the body* (2 Corinthians 5:10). It is also important to realize that the ultimate goal of salvation according to Paul is not the saving of the soul, but rather as he wrote in Romans 8:29, "to be conformed to the image of his Son."

3. *Salvation is a process.* Just as salvation is more than saving the soul, so it is more than a "once-and-for-all" point in time. The question, "Are you saved?" is a good one. All preaching should be directed toward decision. But the question, "Are you saved?" is incomplete. In a review of the word "saved" in the New Testament, one finds that salvation is a process. Christians *will be* saved (Romans 5:9, 10). Christians *were* saved (Romans 8:24). Christians are *being* saved (1 Corinthians 1:18). Paul wrote about the gospel by which you *are* saved (1 Corinthians 15:2), and about the gospel by which you *have been* saved (Ephesians 2:5). Salvation is past, present, and future! Paul said, "For salvation is nearer to us now than when we first believed" (Romans 13:11).

Christians experience salvation in different ways. For some it begins with great suddenness; for others it comes gradually. The believers' church stresses the importance of coming to new life in Jesus Christ. But that's not all. Salvation is a lifelong matter.

Salvation is a pilgrimage. Christians are strangers passing through this world. They live day by day in Christ and walk in His Spirit. By His power they do not fulfill the lust of the flesh. The question, "Are you saved?" is not enough. "Do you know Jesus and are you following Him as a part of His church?" is a better question.

CHAPTER 7

Baptism

A good point to begin a discussion of the Anabaptist view of baptism is with the Schleitheim Confession, the earliest Anabaptist statement of faith. Here is the first of seven articles:

"Notice concerning baptism. Baptism shall be given to all those who have been taught repentance and amendment of life and [who] believe truly that their sins are taken away through Christ, and to all those who desire to walk in the resurrection of Jesus Christ and be buried with Him in death, so that they might rise with Him; to all those who with such an understanding themselves desire and request it from us. . . ." The next section repudiates infant baptism.

Many phrases of importance are found in this statement. It refers to the congregation *teaching* those who are to be baptized. It mentions the *amendment of life* of the person to be baptized. It alludes to the ongoing nature of the Christian life, *to walk in the resurrection*.

In essence, baptism is the means through which the reborn believer commits himself or herself to a life of obedience, in the fellowship with other believers, and is enrolled in the visible community of salvation. Hubmaier made the point that baptism is enrollment in the visible community. The nature of the church, the nature of salvation, and the nature of the Christian life are involved in the Anabaptist/Mennonite understanding of baptism.

Before going further here are a few Anabaptist/Mennonite emphases about baptism.

1. *Baptism is administered to a believer, not on the basis of what he knows, but as the Scriptures and the historic Mennonite faith indicate, on the evidences of the new life.* When a person is baptized, he doesn't *know* all there is to know. Those who have been Christians for many years, don't know all there is to know about Jesus Christ and the gospel, though knowing is an important dimension. Knowledge is not the main criterion for baptism. Rather, the evidence of new birth and life in the Spirit are essential for baptism. This idea bears on the baptism of children. Anabaptists believed that children do not have need of the new birth until, like Adam and Eve, they choose evil. Thus baptism is administered only to those in whom the gift of rebirth is evident.

2. *Concerning baptism, Anabaptists differ significantly from much of Protestantism, as well as Roman Catholicism, not only by not baptizing babies, but also by the importance given to baptism when compared to other practices of the church.*

In general, both the Catholic Church (in the mass) and Protestant churches give much more attention to communion than to baptism. However, among Anabaptists baptism had first place because baptism is the critical issue in realizing a regenerate, disciplined church. Baptism is to be administered only to those who are able to covenant (or to pledge themselves) to God and His church. The concept of the Christian life as a pilgrimage makes baptism important. Christians are on the way. This concept of the church is quite different from Corpus Christianum, in which all the people are members by birth and infant baptism. Such a church emphasizes communion, because it thinks of itself as pardoned, and feasting on the manna, rather than on a pilgrimage concerned with crossing the Red Sea. Paul spoke of baptism in the terminology of being baptized in the sea (1 Corinthians 10:1-5).

3. *Baptism is the tool for gathering a redeemed society, a society of pilgrims, separated from the evil of the unregenerated world.* So important was baptism to the early Anabaptists that Hubmaier said, "Where there is no proper baptism, there is no church." This was not a reference to "baptismal regeneration." Rather, the emphasis was on the essential nature of the new birth and the pilgrim life. Baptism was an open commitment to and confession of both the experience of new life and of being on the way. Baptism was always entered into freely. No one was coerced. It was received on the basis of one's own desire.

4. *Baptism is the symbol of discontinuity with the world.* At baptism one breaks with the past and commits oneself to Jesus Christ and to His people. It's hard to imagine how baptism and circumcision were connected in some theologies. For some it seemed logical that just as baby boys were circumcised in Israel and became part of the people, so babies were now baptized and became part of the church. The two symbols, however, are quite different. Baptism means discontinuity with the past and openness to a new future. Circumcision implies continuity with a people. Thus the two symbols go in different directions.

5. *In terms of binding and loosing, some have seen bap-*

tism as "binding," and discipline as "loosing." A person enters the community by baptism and binds himself to fellow believers. However, if a believer falls into sin and continues in a rebellious way, he is disciplined or loosed.

6. *At the heart of baptism is a pledge—a pledge to the Father, to the Son, to the Holy Spirit, and to fellow believers to live a pilgrim life of discipleship.* Baptism has nothing to do with removing "original sin" nor does it in a miraculous way convey grace or regeneration. Baptism is entry into the visible church.

Just as some citizens of the United States pledge allegiance to the flag, so believers pledge allegiance to Christ's kingdom. In the days of the Anabaptists, citizens were required to take an oath of allegiance to the city in which they lived. The Anabaptists refused to take such an oath because, they said, they had made their promise to God in baptism!

7. *Baptism is a symbol; it is not a sacrament.* It is an ordinance, and as an ordinance it is basically a teaching device. But what does baptism symbolize? This has given rise to an unfortunate detour in the life of the church. For some reason, the church has frequently argued about the mode of baptism while often missing its meaning. Historically, there have been two ways to baptize: immersion and pouring or sprinkling.

Actually neither mode can carry all the symbolism. Immersion symbolizes participation in the death, burial, and resurrection of Jesus. The believer is immersed in the water and then raised out of the water. But with immersion has gone many other questions: How is it done? Is the believer immersed forward or backward? Is the believer immersed once or three times?

Pouring symbolizes Pentecost and the pouring out of the Spirit. In pouring, the one to be baptized kneels, and after

the water is administered, he is offered the right hand of
fellowship and is lifted to a standing position with the words,
"As Christ was raised from the dead even so are you raised
into newness of life." Rising from the knees carries the symbolism of resurrection. In both modes water symbolizes
washing away of sin.

But more important than these symbols in Mennonite
theology is the understanding that baptism is a symbol of
brotherhood. Historically, whether landowner or peasant,
whether patrician or servant, whether master or apprentice,
all are baptized together.

For 400 years 1 John 5:8, "There are three witnesses, the
Spirit, the water, and the blood, and these three agree," has
been a basic text for Anabaptist preaching about baptism.
Unfortunately, I was middle-aged before I knew this. I discovered it first in Ethelbert Stauffer's *The Anabaptist
Theology of Martyrdom.*[1] Then when reading Roland
Armour's *Anabaptist Baptism* (Herald Press, 1966) it's
surprising to see how often this verse is mentioned in connection with baptism—by Hubmaier, Marpeck, and Hut—
to name a few. To discuss baptism using 1 John 5:8 is to be
on biblical, as well as historic ground. There are three witnesses: the Spirit, the water, and the blood. And these three
agree.

Behind the administration of baptism stands the church
that administers the ordinance. In the 1 John text there is a
sequence. Water baptism is seen at the center of redemptive
history. First, there was death to sin through the working of
the Spirit. Then water baptism was administered in the
midst of the congregation. All of this looks forward to the future—to participation in salvation and to the final baptism

---

1. *The Mennonite Quarterly Review*, Vol. XIX, No. 3; pp. 180-214.

when the believer enters into the next life and resurrection. The ordinance of water baptism supported the inner testimony of the Spirit and the outer testimony of blood. Those being baptized leave the old order of sin and death and enter new life and salvation.

A well-known baptismal hymn refers to a "great transaction."[2] This is an important word for understanding baptism. Baptism is essentially a transaction. At baptism persons not only confess their faith and enter into the visible church, but other believers acknowledge that they indeed recognize the presence of the Spirit in the life of the person being baptized. At baptism the one baptized *gives* a testimony, and he also *receives* a testimony from the congregation. There is this dual nature to each of these witnesses.

1. *The witness of the Spirit.* This is the gift of salvation. In the life of the one baptized, the witness of the Spirit means cleansing from sin, power to overcome sin, and the initial transformation of character or the new birth. This is the inner baptism which enables a person to will to live a holy life.

But among the Anabaptists the testimony of the one baptized was not enough. The additional testimony of the congregation was needed. It was not enough for a person to come to the congregation and say, "I have received the Holy Spirit." The claim had to be authenticated by brothers and sisters, who could say, "Yes, we see the work of the Spirit in your life."

A problem facing the church today is unauthenticated claims of professing Christians. Historically, baptism did not follow immediately upon confession of faith. Some refer to

---

2. Philip Doddridge, 1755, in "Happy Day": " 'Tis done, the great transaction's done; I am my Lord's and He is mine."

the story of the Ethiopian eunuch in Acts 8 as an indication
that baptism should follow immediately upon confession of
faith. There are one or two other illustrations like this in
Acts. But from church history it becomes clear that this was
not the general practice. The church was a persecuted community. Immediate' baptism would have made it easy for
persecutors to enter the church, to destroy it or to identify
members. The very life of the church demanded that
members authenticate the claims of persons desiring to unite
with the congregation.

Furthermore, early congregations sensed the importance
of teaching. History also shows how seriously teaching was
taken in the early church. To teach the one to be baptized
was an important congregational responsibility. It also en-
abled the congregation to identify the work of the Spirit in
the life of the one to be baptized. Thus in connection with
baptism, the witness of the Spirit implied this transaction:
the one to be baptized witnessed to the Spirit in his life, and
the congregation confirmed that the Spirit was indeed working in that person's life.

2. *The witness of water.* At water baptism the believer announced publicly a desire to fellowship with the church. As
the believer acknowledged publicly that he was a brother or
sister in Christ, the congregation also publicly acknowledged
the new believer as one with them.

At water baptism there was an oral confession of faith.
The one being baptized publicly stated: "I believe in God. I
believe in Jesus Christ. I believe in the Holy Spirit. I am
sorry for my sins. I promise to live a life of faithfulness to
Jesus Christ until death." In addition to the oral confession
of faith and the promise of faithfulness, there was a transaction that today is often ignored. The one being baptized
placed himself in the care, discipline, and fellowship of the

faithful community. But even this was not enough. The congregation also pledged to the one being baptized their love, care, and discipline.

For 150 years (until 1960) the Brethren in Christ included this in their baptismal vows[3]: "Do you promise that if any of your brethren or sisters should trespass against you, you will go and tell them their faults between them and you alone as taught in Matthew 18:15, 16? Inasmuch as we are all fallible, if you should trespass against any of your brethren or sisters and they would come and tell you of your fault (according to Matthew 18), are you willing to receive it?" In this transaction new members and the congregation solemnly covenanted to submit to mutual discipline. A visible church binds and loosens. Without this mutual love and concern, to belong or not to belong to the church scarcely matters.

At water baptism individual and congregational purity are united. At baptism both the one baptized and the congregation pledge to each other and to God to live according to the rule of Christ.

3. *The witness of blood.* This was the pledge of continued yieldedness to Christ and the church. The witness of blood had two meanings. On one hand, the Christian life was seen as a constant struggle against sin. Blood was the symbol of that struggle—a serious bloody struggle. On the other was the reality of persecution and martyrdom. The faithful church across the centuries has faced persecution and death.

Among the Anabaptists two German words were especially important: *Bussfertigkeit*—which meant continued repentance (this is in harmony with the concept of salvation

---

3. Ronald J. Sider, "Spare the Rod and Spoil the Church," *Eternity*, October 1976, p. 19.

as a process—believers were saved, are being saved, and will be saved); and *Gelassenheit*—which meant a continued submission and surrender to God.

The Anabaptists saw these two meanings in the witness of blood: (1) a continuing struggle with sin and (2) constantly facing death because of faithfulness. In this they followed the example of Jesus. Immediately after baptism Jesus was taken into the wilderness. There He faced a life-and-death struggle with sin. When Jesus spoke about His martyrdom on the cross He asked, "Are you able to drink the cup that I drink or to be baptized with the baptism with which I am baptized?" (Mark 10:38); "I have a baptism to be baptized with" (Luke 12:50). Thus in the witness of blood—the struggle with sin, and the readiness to face martyrdom and death—was the transaction of new member and congregation promising each other to struggle with sin unto death. When a believer was killed for the faith, the testimony of the godless was added to the testimony of the congregation that here, indeed, was a child of God!

"There are three witnesses, the Spirit, the water, and the blood, and these three agree." Note it was not the witness of the Spirit alone, nor the witness of water alone, nor the struggle with sin or martyrdom alone. The church has tended to emphasize one and neglect the others, or to make one more important than the others, but John wrote, "These three agree!"

Today the church must recover this profound understanding of baptism.

CHAPTER 8

Breaking of Bread*

A study of one's faith is important, because Christians are influenced by other theological streams. Also, to make the best witness in the world, it is important to know not only in whom one believes, but what one believes.

Theologically, the Anabaptist/Mennonite faith when set beside other theological streams often seems to take ninety-degree turns in meaning, although the vocabulary is quite similar. By way of review, everyone talks about making Jesus central, but how He is made central varies widely. The creeds make Jesus central with "born of the Virgin" and "crucified under Pontius Pilate." The Anabaptists saw Jesus' life and teachings as extremely important, when He is central.

In its understanding of the church, Anabaptist/Mennonite theology takes a significant turn. Both Roman Catholics and the Reformers saw the church as the mass of people, "Christendom," with the true church invisible in the

---

*Breaking of bread is the term used in the *Schleitheim Confession* for the Lord's Supper or communion.

midst of it. Anabaptists saw the church as visible, with binding and loosing being important dimensions of that visibility. To speak of church was to speak of brotherhood, of
those who were born from above.

The meaning of salvation also took another direction. Salvation was vastly more than giving intellectual assent to
propositions and experiencing a subjective inner experience.
Mennonite theology saw salvation as a process. The question, "Are you saved?" was not enough, since the Bible uses
all three tenses—"were saved," "are being saved," and "will
be saved." Salvation involves the totality of one's existence
and relationship with fellow believers.

When it comes to the meaning of baptism, Anabaptists
took another significant turn. They baptized adults. The fact
that they "rebaptized" resulted in the name "Anabaptists."
They saw baptism as the gate to the church. They saw it as a
transactional experience, in which a witness took place. They
referred to 1 John 5:8 and the three witnesses, the Spirit, the
water, and the blood. The one being baptized testified that
the Spirit was at work in the life, and the congregation affirmed that this was the case. The one being baptized gave
allegiance to the congregation and in turn received the congregation's promise of care and support. Together they
pledged to be faithful even unto death, the "witness of
blood."

In "breaking of bread" Mennonite faith took another significant turn. To describe the difference, it is important to
note those passages of Scripture that have been widely used
among Anabaptists to understand the meaning of breaking
of bread.

1. *1 Corinthians 10:14-22.* Here Paul dealt with the question of worshiping idols. In doing so, he made clear some important insights about the nature of breaking bread. Paul

wrote, "I speak as to sensible men; judge for yourselves what I say. The cup of blessing which we bless, is it not a participation [the King James Version uses the word "communion"] in the blood of Jesus Christ? The bread which we break, is it not a participation [or communion] in the body of Christ? Because there is one bread, we who are many are one body, for we all partake of the one bread."

Then Paul went on to show the impossibility of having anything to do with pagan practices, and concluded, "You cannot drink the cup of the Lord and the cup of demons. You cannot partake of the table of the Lord and the table of demons. Shall we provoke the Lord to jealousy? Are we stronger than he?"

From Paul's writing it becomes clear that communion is not an individual matter! The cup of blessing which *we* bless, is it not a participation in the blood of Christ? In the Greek, the word for participation is *koinōnia*. This word means fellowship. The passage could well be translated, "The cup of blessing which *we* bless, is it not *fellowship* in the blood of Christ? The bread which *we* break, is it not *fellowship* in the body of Christ?"

Fellowship is an important New Testament concept. "God is faithful," Paul wrote earlier in this book, "by whom you were called into the fellowship of his Son, Jesus Christ our Lord (1 Corinthians 1:9). Paul used this term when he wrote about the impossibility of being involved with the things of this world. "What fellowship has light with darkness?" (2 Corinthians 6:14; note also 1 Corinthians 10). Paul contrasted Christ and Belial, the believer with the unbeliever, and the temple of God with idols.

To the Philippians Paul wrote that he was thankful for their partnership (another translation of the same word, "fellowship") in the gospel from the first day to now (1:5).

In 1 John are familiar statements about fellowship: "You may have fellowship with us...." "If we say we have fellowship with him while we walk in darkness, we lie and do not live according to the truth; but if we walk in the light, as he is in the light, we have fellowship with one another" (1:3, 6). Fellowship is not an individual matter.

The many become one. "Because there is one bread, we who are many are one body, for we all partake of the one bread" (1 Corinthians 10:17). When Paul wrote about gifts in Romans 12, he pointed out that they were given for the common good. He wrote, "So we, though many, are *one body* in Christ, and individually members one of another" (Romans 12:5). In the same way Paul wrote that there is one bread, and one body. "We who are many are *one body*, for we all partake of the one bread" (1 Corinthians 10:17).

Here is a significant shift from much of Christendom. For many, communion is basically an individual matter. You examine yourself to see if you believe in Christ, to see if you are right with God (vertically), and then you come to the table. But this is not what Paul taught. He saw the corporate dimension of coming to the table. It is a fellowship meal of people who are *one* in Christ.

2. *1 Corinthians 11:17-34*. Generally speaking, in communion services when 1 Corinthians 11 is read before serving the bread and cup, the reading begins at verse 23. "For I received from the Lord what I also delivered to you, that the Lord Jesus on the night when he was betrayed took bread, and when he had given thanks, he broke it, and said, 'This is my body which is for you. Do this in remembrance of me.' For as often as you eat this bread and drink the cup, you proclaim the Lord's death until he comes."

The reading may also include, "Whoever, therefore, eats the bread or drinks the cup of the Lord in an unworthy manner will be guilty of profaning the body and blood of the Lord. Let a man examine himself, and so eat of the bread and drink of the cup. For any one who eats and drinks without discerning the body eats and drinks judgment upon himself."

The striking thing is that when these verses are taken from their context, they give communion a highly individualistic flavor, in which individuals simply remember what Jesus did and examine themselves, and look for His return. However, the Anabaptists did not take this passage from its context, which deals with the problem of congregational unity. "In the following instructions I do not commend you, because when you come together it is not for the better but for the worse. For, in the first place, when you assemble as a church, I hear that there are divisions among you; and I partly believe it, for there must be factions among you in order that those who are genuine among you may be recognized. When you meet together, it is not the Lord's supper that you eat. For in eating, each one goes ahead with his own meal, and one is hungry and another is drunk. What! Do you not have houses to eat and drink in? Or do you despise the church of God and humiliate those who have nothing? What shall I say to you? Shall I commend you in this? No, I will not!" (1 Corinthians 11:17-22).

The fact of the matter is this. If a congregation does not come to breaking of bread in love and unity, they are not partaking of the Lord's Supper! When a congregation eats with a disunited spirit (11:20), they do not eat the Lord's Supper. Then what do they eat?

In 11:18 is the word "divisions." The Greek word *skisma* is root for the English word "schism." In 11:19 is the word "factions." This Greek word *hairesis* is root for the English word "heresy." Strangely enough, this word is almost always translated "sect" in the New Testament. In Acts this word refers to a "sect" of the Pharisees. The Way was a "sect." In Galatians it is translated as "party spirit." Only in 2 Peter 2:1 is the word translated as heresy or incorrect doctrine. In 1 Corinthians 11 the word refers to groups or "sects" within the congregation.

When love is missing, Paul wrote, the observance is not the Lord's Supper! Or when unity is missing, it is not the Lord's Supper! In the case of the Corinthians divisions existed between the rich and poor. The rich were filling their bellies, while the poor were going hungry. In Anabaptist thought, stress was placed on the unity and common commitments of those breaking bread.

3. *John 13:1-17.* In John's Gospel the Lord's Supper is not dealt with as such. However, the events in the upper room are important for understanding its meaning. Early Anabaptist leaders always called attention to the fact that in the upper room Jesus washed His disciples' feet. John did not write about the Last Supper in the same way that Matthew, Mark, and Luke did. Rather, John included the washing of the disciples' feet. It is in that context that Jesus initiated His Supper, and said, "A new commandment I give to you, that you love one another; even as I have loved you, that you also love one another. By this all men will know that you are my disciples, if you have love for one another" (John 13:34).

These three passages with the emphasis on unity, the one loaf, have provided a basis for a different understanding of the Lord's Supper.

For many church groups the question was the nature of the bread and cup. Does the bread actually become the flesh of Jesus? Does the cup actually become the blood of Jesus? Or do they undergo some other kind of change? There were arguments about words—"transubstantiation" and "consubstantiation."

The bread and cup were also called "sacraments." Marpeck and other Anabaptists totally rejected the word sacrament, as though in itself the Supper were some sort of a means of grace. Pilgram Marpeck wrote, "The true meaning of communion is mystified and obscured by the word sacrament." The Anabaptists did not focus on the bread or the cup.

Another common argument revolved around who should administer communion. For many, only persons with proper credentials, with proper succession, and who were properly ordained could give the emblems. Again, Anabaptists were not involved in that argument. They understood that the real concern was not what happened to the emblems, nor who administered communion. Rather, the quality of the lives of the persons who joined in the remembrance and their relations to each other were of supreme importance!

The emphasis does not lie on what the bread and wine should be or contain, but rather in the reason for our participation. But as Pilgram Marpeck wrote, "As members of one body, we proclaim the death of Christ and the bodily union attained by untainted brotherly love."[1]

The meaning of breaking of bread was and still is a gathering of the saints. This gathering is characterized by both faith and love—faith in Jesus, the memory of His cross, broken body, and shed blood, and awaiting His return. But at the same time breaking of bread reflects the love of believers for each other.

The fact is simply this. "Horizontal" unity (Christian love

---

1. William Klassen and Walter Klaassen, *The Writings of Pilgram Marpeck* (Scottdale, Pa.: Herald Press, 1978), p. 284.

for one another) is a confirmation of the "vertical" unity (the faith they profess in God). As one Anabaptist said, "The Lord's Supper cannot be eaten without love."

Thus the judgment Paul described in 1 Corinthians 11 is not the result of taking the bread and the cup that have been mystically changed. Rather, the judgment comes when believers fail to love Jesus wholeheartedly, and fail to love their brothers and sisters just as fully.

"The Lord's Supper is a physical *and loving* gathering or assembly, a communal eating and drinking by Christian believers to proclaim the death of the Lord and to join one another in brotherly love."[2] The demonstration of this love is in their profound concern for each other.

Note what the ancient *Schleitheim Confession* says about breaking bread:

> The ban shall be employed with all those who have given themselves over to the Lord, to walk after Him in His commandments; those who have been baptized into the one body of Christ, and let themselves be called brothers or sisters, and still somehow slip and fall into error and sin, being inadvertently overtaken. The same shall be warned twice privately and the third time be publicly admonished before the entire congregation according to the command of Christ (Matthew 18). But this shall be done according to the ordering of the Spirit of God before the breaking of bread so that we may all in one spirit and in one love break and eat from one bread and drink from one cup.
>
> Concerning the breaking of bread, we have become one and agree thus: all those who desire to break the one bread in remembrance of the broken body of Christ and all those who wish to drink of one drink in remembrance of the shed blood of Christ, *they must beforehand be united in the one body of Christ,* that is the congregation of God, whose head is Christ,

---

2. *Ibid.*, p. 282.

and that by baptism. For as Paul indicates, we cannot be partakers at the same time of the table of the Lord and the table of devils. Nor can we at the same time partake and drink of the cup of the Lord and the cup of devils. That is: all those who have fellowshiped with the dead works of darkness have no part in the light. Thus all who follow the devil and the world, have no part with those who have been called out of the world unto God. . . .

So it shall and must be, that whoever does not share the calling of the one God to one faith, to one baptism, to one spirit, to one body together with all the children of God, may not be made one loaf together with them, as must be true if one wishes truly to break bread according to the command of Christ.[3]

In early Anabaptist preaching the following analogy was used many times. Here are two versions of it:

With the bread the unity among brethren is symbolized. Where there are many small kernels of grain to be combined into one loaf there is need first to grind them and to make them into one flour . . . which can be achieved only through suffering. Just as Christ, our dear Lord, went before us, so too we want to follow him in like manner. And the bread symbolizes the unity of the brotherhood.

Likewise with the wine: many small grapes come together to make the one wine. That happens by means of the press, understood here as suffering. . . . And thus also the wine indicates suffering. Hence, whoever wants to be in brotherly union, has to drink from the cup of the Lord, for this cup symbolizes suffering.[4]

Menno Simons wrote,

Just as natural bread has to be kneaded of many kernels of

---

3. John H. Yoder, trans. and ed., *The Schleitheim Confession* (Scottdale, Pa.: Herald Press, 1977), pp. 10, 11.

4. Robert Friedmann, *The Theology of Anabaptism* (Scottdale, Pa.: Herald Press, 1973), pp. 140, 141.

grain broken in the mill, together with water and then baked by the heat of the fire, in the same way the church of Christ is made up of many believers, broken in their hearts by the mill of God's word, baptized with water by the Holy Spirit, and brought together in one body by pure and unadulterated love at the Lord's table.[5]

So, in the Anabaptist/Mennonite understanding of the Lord's Supper, the observance is not an individual matter. It is a group experience in which there is a profound demonstration of love and a profound concern for the spiritual welfare of one another.

In the last century the ways in which some of these early insights were expressed went to seed. The church lost sight of the need for a deep sense of love and forgiveness. Communion became an occasion and/or method to impose mechanically and at times legalistically church rules and regulations. Because discipline fell into these unacceptable forms the church today tends to shy away from discipline. It is not enough to say, "I take communion because I am right with God," or "because I want to receive a blessing." There must be also a concern for the brother and sister, caring for each other, confronting one another with failures, sins, and shortcomings, and then forgiving and accepting each other in love.

It has been a long time since many congregations have held counsel meetings. Counsel meetings were the last traces of the historic position that Matthew 18 was to be practiced in the life of the congregation, especially before communion.

In the 1978 study document of the Mennonite General Assembly, *Affirming Our Faith in Word and Deed,* is this

---

5. *Ibid.,* p. 141.

statement, "Those who break bread in remembrance of the broken body of Jesus Christ and those who drink the one drink in remembrance of the shed blood must be united beforehand in the one body of Christ (1 Corinthians 11:17-32). Those who partake examine themselves (1 Corinthians 11:28). They are also open to their brothers and sisters for admonition and correction because they take seriously the warning of Paul about drinking the cup of the Lord and the cup of devils (1 Corinthians 10:21). In the historic view of breaking bread, neither the nature nor the meaning of the bread and the cup, nor the status of the one officiating is the point of concern. The concern is with the community— those who take part, that all should share the one calling of God, the one faith, the one baptism, the one Spirit, and thus be made the one loaf together (1 Corinthians 10:17)."[6]

A pressing question before the church is this: Do we want to recover the historic affirmations about breaking bread, or will we be most comfortable continuing an evangelical, individualistic, vertical understanding of the Lord's Supper?

---

6. Published by Mennonite Publishing House, Scottdale, Pa., 1978, p. 43.

CHAPTER 9

Worship and Proclamation

When the eleven disciples went to Galilee to the mountain that Jesus directed, they saw Him, and they *worshiped* Him! Then it was that Jesus gave the *"Great Commission"* (Matthew 28:16-20). The disciples were to go and to make disciples of all nations. Worship and proclamation go hand in hand and are deeply interrelated.

I'm not happy when the word "celebration" is used as a synonym for worship. Worship is a much better word choice, and is widely understood. Millard Lind in his book makes the point that celebration is too broad a term, because it does not help to distinguish between Christian celebration and non-Christian celebration.[*]

Christians celebrate, whether personally or corporately, the rule of God. The rule of God is what makes worship meaningful. The rule of God, as experienced in the new community, is demonstrated, proclaimed, and enforced as

---

[*]Millard C. Lind, *Biblical Foundations for Christian Worship* (Scottdale, Pa.: Herald Press, 1973), p. 5.

the deeds of God are told—deeds of the past, the present, and the future.

Sunday morning worship services should have a time for members to share experiences, concerns, needs, and insights. There is a sense in which preaching and teaching, based on the Old and New Testaments, declare again and again God's acts in the past. As members share in testimonies and prayers, they rehearse the acts of God in the present.

It has always been customary for the people of God to assemble. In the Old Testament, Israel camped with their tents around the tabernacle. In a sense, life was one large assembly or "church service" with the tabernacle serving as the focal point for the entire life of the community. The church has always encouraged assembly. When congregations meet today, they are part of a historic action that stretches across the centuries.

When the people of God come together, historically and in the present, at least seven things occur.

1. *There are creedal statements.* This does not refer to the recitation of the Nicene Creed or the Apostles' Creed, or other forms that have worked their way into worship services. Fundamentally, when the congregation gathered, the profound, exclusive, and inclusive statement was made, "Jesus is Lord!" There are many references in the New Testament to this basic creedal statement. Paul wrote, "If you confess with your lips that Jesus is Lord and believe in your heart that God raised him from the dead, you will be saved" (Romans 10:9). That Jesus is Lord is at the heart of Christian faith.

Paul wrote, "No one can say 'Jesus is Lord' except by the Holy Spirit" (1 Corinthians 12:3). In Philippians, at the climax of the great hymn, are the words, "at the name of Jesus every knee should bow . . . and every tongue confess

that Jesus Christ is Lord, to the glory of God the Father"
(2:10, 11).

For the congregation to say, "Jesus is Lord," is much like
the Old Testament congregation repeating the first commandment, "You shall have no other gods before me"
(Exodus 20:3). "Jesus is Lord" is the New Testament
equivalent of the first commandment, but it goes much
further in that Jesus made God fully known.

To say, "Jesus is Lord," is a positive statement. At the
same time it has a negative dimension, in denying that there
are other lords. This makes worship a threatening political
act. Thus when Christians in any country of the world
confess Jesus as Lord, they are in effect saying that all other
authorities take second place. This is why Christianity is
usually opposed in totalitarian states. Dictators are keenly
aware of this disloyalty, since Christians acknowledge only
one Sovereign, and that is Jesus. He reigns supreme. He is
the One to whom they give allegiance totally and fully. This
fundamental, creedal statement has made Christians aliens,
pilgrims, and strangers on the face of the earth.

This insight that was in the minds and hearts of Ana-
baptists/Mennonites nine or ten generations ago when they
left Switzerland to worship as they saw fit in the new world,
must be reaffirmed in our time. The alien and stranger concepts are both implicit and explicit aspects of making Jesus
Lord. They must be emphasized in both proclamation and
celebration today.

In the midst of political speeches and patriotic holiday addresses that stress the ultimacy of fatherland and militarism,
it is good to assemble as Christians to make the profound
eternal proclamation, "Jesus is Lord!"

2. *There is singing.* Christians have always been joyful.
Many hymns of the early church are recorded in the New

Testament. Unfortunately, because of the way type is set in the King James and many other versions, poetry is often difficult to identify. Philippians 2:6-11 contains a great hymn of the church. In 1 Timothy 3:16 is found another:

> Great, indeed, we confess is the mystery of our religion:
> He was manifested in the flesh,
> vindicated in the spirit,
> seen by angels,
> preached among the nations,
> believed on in the world,
> taken up in glory.

Ephesians 5:14 is a baptismal hymn:

> Awake, O sleeper, and arise from the dead,
> and Christ shall give you light.

3. *There is preaching.* Preaching has always been an important part of worship. In recent times, it seems, preaching has been downgraded. However, for the welfare of the church, the importance of preaching must be recaptured. It seems that conferences are held for ministers on counseling, education, evangelism, administration—on everything but the central task of preaching!

It is interesting to note how much preaching has been preserved in the text of the New Testament. Though the Book of Acts traces the missionary journeys of Paul, the real thrust of the book is in the sermons. Peter's sermon at Pentecost is tremendously important. His sermons preached after Pentecost are recorded in Acts 3 and 11. Look at the amount of space given Stephen's sermon (Acts 7). At least three of Paul's sermons are recorded in Acts 13, 17, and 20. Preaching was a central task. Remember, the teachings of Jesus were also brought together in the form of a sermon (Matthew 5, 6, and 7) for use in the life of congregations.

4. *There is prayer.* Acts records some of the prayers of the early church. For example, there was the prayer of boldness (Acts 4:24-30), and prayer for imprisoned Peter (Acts 12:5).

5. *There is baptism and the breaking of bread.* The thrust of these was discussed earlier.

6. *There is exhortation, teaching, and admonition of one another.*

7. *There is brotherly address (Matthew 18), binding, and loosing.*

The life of the church is more than assembly. James made the point, "Religion that is pure and undefiled before God and the Father is this: to visit orphans and widows in their affliction, and to keep oneself unstained from the world" (James 1:27).

Worship and proclamation of the gospel go hand in hand. As noted earlier in Matthew 28:17-20, the disciples worshiped Jesus, and then He gave them the commission to go into all the world.

Proclamation is the point at which faith is tested. It is in proclamation that Christians discover whether their faith has credibility or not. Through proclamation of the gospel persons are born into the kingdom. Through proclamation persons grow like Jesus. Further, proclamation keeps faith honest, since unsubstantiated claims for the gospel undermine the effectiveness of proclamation.

Proclamation keeps faith intelligible. Proclamation forces Christians to explain the faith without theological jargon. Proclamation is more than repeating the pious words. To say a word does not necessarily convey a reality. Frequent use of words like justification, sanctification, and regeneration may confuse rather than clarify.

Proclamation is likely the church's weakest point. Here are seven reasons why the church is weak in proclamation.

1. *The drive for respectability.* Many are concerned about what people in the community think of the congregation. Consequently, members don't want to talk about the implications of making Jesus Lord as it relates to government, to militarism, to economic practices. Often the search for financial security keeps Christians quiet about business ethics.

2. *Willingness to let others do the work.* This deadens a sense of personal responsibility. To give money so that others can serve seems to suffice.

3. *A deep-seated uncertainty about the importance of proclamation.* The feeling is that proclamation is an optional matter. It is done if time permits or if an opportunity arises. This uncertainty has given rise to a pseudo-intellectualism where Christians spend time discussing issues related to proclamation—are missions the right thing to do? Is it proper to tamper with the cultures of others? Is Christianity superior to other religions? Such discussions become substitutes for action and often fail to take seriously the fundamental affirmation of the apostles, "There is no name under heaven given among men by which we must be saved" (Acts 4:12). This is both the scandal and the essence of Christianity. Jesus is Lord. There is no other. He was given all authority and He told His followers to go into all the world and make disciples of all peoples.

4. *A tendency to polarize between "home" and "abroad."* In United States there is a trend away from involvement overseas. On radio talk programs there is constant criticism of sending government monies overseas for aid or development. There is a tendency today to think locally rather than worldwide. The center of the world is where I am!

This is also happening in the church. Some say, "It's no use to send missionaries. There's too much to be done at home." In the Book of Acts the concern went in the opposite direction. Wherever Christians were, they were moving on—from Jerusalem, to Judea, to Samaria, and finally to the ends of the earth. Christianity is always an outward movement.

5. *Proclamation has become professionalized.* This is the job of the preacher, the evangelist, or the missionary—persons especially trained to do it. The New Testament knows nothing of this. Basically, the New Testament sees proclamation as dependent upon the call of the Lord and the support of the congregation.

6. *Concerns for self-fulfillment have blunted the concern for discipleship.* Today, feelings are important. The key question seems to be "How do you feel?" There is nothing wrong with an emotional experience of Christianity. Thank God for emotions. But Jesus did not call persons to self-centered spirituality! He calls to self-denial, to love for God, and to love for neighbor.

7. *Easy forms of obedience are substituted for the hard realities of the cross.* Proclamation is difficult. The congregation hesitates to ask members to do difficult tasks. But here again it is important to see how Jesus faced the cross. Jesus went to the cross because He knew it was God's will for Him, and because beyond the cross was joy, "who for the joy that was set before him endured the cross, despising the shame, and is seated at the right hand of the throne of God" (Hebrews 12:2).

Perhaps Christians are weak in proclamation because they want joy this side of the cross, when the joy is on the other side! Joy is in knowing and in doing the will of God! Clearly, worship issues in proclamation!

CHAPTER 10

Teaching and Serving

Teaching and serving often appear together in the New Testament. In the upper room before the crucifixion, Jesus reaffirmed His role as a teacher and also washed His disciples' feet as a servant (John 13:13-16). When Paul listed the gifts of persons to the church, he noted that the work of pastor/teachers was the equipping of the saints for the work of ministry [or service] (Ephesians 4:12).

Jesus held teaching and witnessing together. He seemed to suggest that one without the other was not enough. In what is called the Great Commission, Jesus was very explicit. His disciples were to *make disciples* and also were to *teach them to observe* all that He commanded (Matthew 28:19, 20). Though the focus in this chapter is on teaching and serving, at the outset it is important to note that teaching also goes hand in hand with making disciples (evangelism).

First, some observations about teaching.

1. *Time and again the importance of following Jesus has been emphasized.* "Follow me," Jesus said. To follow Him is to take seriously what He took seriously. To be a teacher and

to teach was at the heart of His personality and action. "You call me teacher.... You are right, for so I am." Clearly, the church takes its cues for the *importance* of teaching, *what* is taught, and *how* to teach from Jesus.

2. *In the church adults are to be taught—those who have decided to become disciples of Jesus.* This cuts across the popular notion that in the church teaching is for children. It is important to teach children in the midst of the congregation, to share with them the data of the faith, to help them grasp the history, the present life, and the destiny of the people of God. However, to teach children requires an informed, practicing group of adult disciples. In fact, children's curriculum materials are really prepared for adults, so that they can share the faith with children.

Children's education tends to focus on the future. The church wants to prepare children for the time they are older and ready to assume leadership in the church. Long ago leaders of the Sunday school movement saw the Sunday school as the "nursery" or "seedbed" of the church. Seeds sown in childhood, it was thought, would grow into strong trees in the future. This perspective was inadequate for several reasons:

First, children's education requires that they have models of discipleship at every stage across the life span. The church must focus on teaching adults to observe all that Jesus commanded, so that children will become aware both of what Jesus taught and how it is expressed in life, as adults provide examples.

Second, though future usefulness appears as a worthy goal, yet Christian education must also focus on the here and now. The present is important because the church must be discerning the will and way of the Lord of the church *now.* The preacher of Hebrews emphasized the importance of "today." Obedience in each "today" is the key to the future of the church.

Third, if Christian education is primarily for children, then as children approach maturity they will not have time for the church's teaching ministry. After all, how can they best demonstrate maturity? By putting away childish things! At the time Christian teaching is most needed, youth follow the examples of those adults who feel little or no need to study deeply the Scriptures, the beliefs, and the practices of the Christian community.

That teaching should focus on adults is clear from the pattern of Jesus. He chose twelve adults to be with Him, not a group of ten-year-olds. Following Him affected every area of their existence. In a similar way, from the community of faith flows Jesus' teaching relating to all areas of life. Relationship to Jesus and His community affects one's business life and family life.

3. *Strong teaching in the congregation contributes to strong Christian homes.* It is important to observe that Jesus called His disciples away from their homes to the upper room, to observe the Last Supper. This was quite different from the observance of Passover, a Jewish home ritual. The upper room setting was essential to a voluntary believers' church, which takes precedence over all other relationships. Were the church primarily ethnic in nature, the rites and practices of the church would be family-oriented.

If participation in the church requires leaving the biological family, this choice must be made. However, as Jesus pointed out, when the disciple does this, he or she receives a new family and a new home. It is in the context of the new community of believing adults that teaching becomes important, as believers teach and admonish one another. Among the believers are the resources needed to enable them to function as followers of Jesus, not only because of the experiences and insights of the believers but also because of the gifts of the Holy Spirit.

If families of believers are to live as Christians, the issues of family life must be dealt with in the congregation. Paul's instructions about marriage and family were not addressed to families. They were addressed to congregations first of all. Strong Christian families spring from strong congregations.

4. *"Church and Sunday school"—both are needed.* A word should be said about the present program for teaching adults. Most congregations have church *and* Sunday school. It is not the purpose here to discuss the historical accidents that have led to this division, nor to complain about the inadequacies of it. When the congregation gathers, adults need both proclamation and interaction. Preaching, without teaching and admonishing one another, is not enough. Unfortunately, in present practices, preaching generally develops one theme while teaching develops another. As a result, what is preached is not dealt with responsibly by the congregation. And in Sunday school class discussions, adequate theological input is often lacking. In neither the Sunday school nor the church part is there sufficient time or opportunity to work toward consensus or decision. These shortcomings could be overcome if the time the congregation is together is seen (and planned for) holistically.

5. *The New Testament church used two teaching methods above all others: (1) transmission of content and (2) providing examples or models.*

Much of Jesus' teaching was brought together in an easily transmitted form—the sermon. See Matthew 5 through 7. Often Jesus referred to Old Testament materials and gave them a new interpretation. Paul frequently used the words "receive" and "deliver" (1 Corinthians 11:23; 15:3). The truth Paul received, he passed on or delivered. In the early church, in both preaching and teaching, there was concern to transmit the truth. That truth was transmitted in at least six areas: the Old Testament, the words of Jesus, doctrines, standards of morality, how to carry on the life of the church, and how to share the faith.

For the church, truth has always been more than words. It must also be lived. In a sense this was the reason for the incarnation. For God to be known by humans, He had to come in human form. Statements about God were not enough. Thus, if the truth of the gospel is to be fully taught, it must be modeled in the lives of disciples. Jesus said, "Every one when he is fully taught will be like his teacher" (Luke 6:40). Modeling went hand in hand with Jesus' preaching and teaching. This is why, as noted earlier, Jesus chose twelve disciples to be with Him. Constantly, He provided the Twelve with an example.

The Father provided a model for His Son, Jesus. John wrote that what the Father does, the Son does likewise (John 5:19). Jesus said that His words and works were learned from the Father (John 9:4; 10:32, 37, 38). In His own case, Jesus believed that the student becomes like his teacher, for Jesus said that He had become like the Father. "He who has seen me has seen the Father" (John 14:9).

This was also true of Jesus and His disciples. He provided an example for them. They were to wash one another's feet (John 13:15); they were to love as He loved them (John 15:12). As He was sent, so they were sent (John 20:21). As He forgave, so they were to forgive (Colossians 3:13).

In turn, the disciples were to provide examples for those who came to faith through their ministry. Paul also understood this. Constantly, he referred to his role as a model— "Follow me, as I follow Christ," "Be imitators of me" (1

Corinthians 4:6, 16; 11:1; Philippians 3:17; 4:9).

Providing models continues to this day as an effective way to teach. Believers are to provide models of discipleship for others, so that all may grow like Jesus. This is in line with Anabaptist Hans Denck's insight, "No one may truly know Christ except one who follows Him in life."

The importance of modeling places great responsibility upon the adults of the congregation. They must provide examples for new believers and for children of what disciples of Jesus are like. This is one reason why busing large numbers of children to Sunday school is only half a program. Provision must also be made for each child to have meaningful contacts and interactions with believing adults. In almost every case, children who have been invited to Sunday school from homes in which parents were not believers, and who have become part of the church as adults, have had adult believers who stood by them through adolescence and early adulthood.

And now some observations about service:

As noted earlier, the work of pastor/teachers was to equip persons for service. Service also implies servanthood. Jesus took the role of a servant. He washed His disciples' feet and instructed His disciples to do likewise.

1. *The posture of the servant is obedience and submission.* This posture is increasingly looked upon with disfavor in today's society. The emphasis is upon doing one's thing. If it feels good, do it! Rather than trying to know and do the will of God, almost any action is justified by the question, "Why not?" The desire is to be served, to climb to positions of power where one can rule, rather than to obey and to submit.

But Jesus beckons His followers in another direction. His experience was one of downward mobility. Though equal with God, He became human. As a human He took the station of a servant. He became obedient—even unto death. His downward mobility, however, led to exaltation. Jesus also calls His followers to downward mobility. Such death, He said, leads to life; whereas upward mobility (life in the world's sense) leads ultimately to death.

2. *Modeling and serving go hand in hand.* How can one better demonstrate what it means to follow Jesus than to be a servant? Jesus' servanthood opened channels to persons from every walk of life, from poverty to riches, from all kinds of backgrounds, and with all kinds of needs. As Jesus served, many opportunities were opened to minister to persons and to share the love of God. Thus serving becomes an expression of making Jesus central as described in chapter 1. Serving is not something tacked on to Anabaptist/Mennonite faith. It is a way of life among those who take Jesus seriously—who believe that His life as a servant is to be expressed in life today. But serving is not done simply to provide models. Rather, it is spontaneous and not self-conscious—the result of love and the promptings of the Holy Spirit.

3. *Placing educating and serving together may provide a clue for the church's teaching ministry.* For too long church leaders in education have tended to listen to and follow educators in public education. Their problems, methods, and prescriptions have been adopted by church educators, often without question. An indicator that a church educator is really on his toes is if he can cite the latest findings of nonchurch educators, and even criticize the church's program in the light of these findings.

However, to take seriously the Scriptures, the nature and history of the people of God, the person, life, work, and teachings of Jesus, and the power and guidance of the Holy

Spirit, it becomes clear that rays of hope come from the church's own foundation and historical turning points. They also provide a base for evaluating the perception of the problems, the methods, and presuppositions of the nonchurch educators.

By bringing together serving and teaching, the traditional separations of the church—between children and adults, ordained and nonordained, spiritual gifts and organizational power, secular and religious, school and life—may be overcome. For serving cannot be divided into weekday and Sunday parts and it makes no distinctions as to whom is served. And teaching occurs as much in the daily round of activities as in school. Serving and teaching are authentic responses to Jesus' call to follow Him. Together they offer hope for realizing new methods, new learnings, and new directions.

CHAPTER 11

Discerning

There is much talk about discernment in the church these days. But it seems that those who use the term most often have not taken the time to examine how the Scriptures use this word, and the work of discernment in the church. Frankly, the New Testament has more to say about discernment than is generally realized.

In English translations of the Bible many words, such as "judge," "determine," "discern," "decide," "esteem," "approve," and "allow" go back to two Greek words: *krino*, which means to judge, to decide, or to assess; and *dokimazo*, which means to be watching or alert. These definitions contribute to an understanding of discernment—to judge, to assess, to watch, and to be alert.

Here are some of the key passages dealing with discernment:

Romans 12:2, 3, NIV, is quite familiar: "Do not conform any longer to the pattern of this world, but be transformed by the renewing of your mind. Then you will be able to test and approve what God's will is—his good, pleasing and

perfect will." This is both the essence and task of discernment, "to test and approve *(dokimazo)* what God's will is."

Romans 14:3, 4, 10, 13. "Let not him who eats despise
him who abstains, and let not him who abstains pass judgment *(krino)* on him who eats.... Who are you to pass
judgment *(krino)* on the servant of another?... Why do you
pass judgment *(krino)* on your brother? Or you, why do you
despise your brother?... Then let us no more pass judgment *(krino)* on one another, but rather decide never to put
a stumbling block or hindrance in the way of a brother.

Romans 14:22. "The faith that you have, keep between
yourself and God; happy is he who has no reason to judge
(krino) himself for what he approves *(dokimazo)*." Here
judgment and approval are exercised on matters that are dis-
putable. The question was whether Christians should be
vegetarians or eat meat, and whether or not they should observe religious holidays. Paul dealt with how Christians
should relate to one another when they disagree.
Disagreements were not to disrupt the corporate life of the
community.

1 Corinthians 6:1-8. Here two church members were in
disagreement. Instead of bringing their dispute to the
brotherhood for discernment, they went to the courts. The
dispute between brothers became public knowledge, and it
was aired before unbelievers. When this happened, Paul
asked, "Can it be that there is no man among you wise
enough to decide *(diakrino)* between members of the
brotherhood, but brother goes to law against brother, and
that before unbelievers?" The implied answer to Paul's
question is simply, "Yes, there are brethren within the congregation that are able to help those in disagreement, to
discern the way to resolve conflict."

1 Corinthians 1:28-32. When preparing to participate in

communion believers are to examine themselves and discern. "Let a man examine himself *(dokimazo)*, and so eat of the bread and drink of the cup. For any one who eats and drinks without discerning *(diakrino)* the body eats and drinks judgment upon himself. . . . But if we judged *(diakrino)* ourselves truly, we should not be judged *(krino)*. But when we are judged *(krino)* by the Lord, we are chastened so that we may not be condemned along with the world."

Quite often the New Testament calls Christians to examine themselves and each other. This activity is to be carried on in the light of the judgment to come, which Paul calls the "day of Christ" (Philippians 1:10). The point is, Christians are to discern because they are living under God who is also discerning. God's discernment and Christian discernment are to coincide. Christians are to live so that they are approved now and also in the judgment.

Ephesians 5:10, 11. This passage uses the familiar terms "put off" and "put on." Christians are to live now in the light of the wrath to come. Paul wrote that Christians were once in darkness, but now they are in the light in the Lord. Then Paul added, "And try to learn what is pleasing to the Lord. Take no part in the unfruitful works of darkness, but instead expose them." An important function of discernment is to help Christians live holy and righteous lives.

Philippians 1:8-11. Here is a remarkable prayer for the believers at Philippi. "And it is my prayer that your love may abound more and more, with knowledge and all *discernment,* so that you may approve what is excellent, and may be pure and blameless for the day of Christ, filled with the fruits of righteousness which come through Jesus Christ, to the glory and praise of God." Note that the words "knowledge" and "discernment" lead to approval (*dokimazo*). Believers are to be pure and blameless—in the light of the day of Christ. Paul also referred to the fruit of righteousness which comes through Jesus Christ. This brings to mind John 15:4, 5, where Jesus spoke about the vine and the branches, and how those who abide in Him bear fruit.

1 Thessalonians 5:15-21. Generally, people think of these verses as a collection of mottoes like: "See that none of you repays evil for evil." "Rejoice always." "Pray constantly." "Give thanks in all circumstances." Verses 19-21, however, make it clear that this is more than a collection of mottoes, for it represents Paul's way of thinking that appears elsewhere (for example, 1 Corinthians 14, where Paul dealt with the question of speaking in tongues and of prophesying in public meetings, and in 1 Thessalonians and in 1 Corinthians, where Paul addressed problems growing out of gifts). So to the Thessalonians Paul wrote, "Do not quench the Spirit, do not despise prophesying, but test everything; hold fast what is good, abstain from every form of evil."

The same problems exist in congregations today. There are members who are impressed or excited about ecstatic manifestations of the Holy Spirit. In effect Paul wrote to those in the congregation who are not charismatic, "Don't quench the Spirit." To those who are charismatic, he wrote, "Do not despise prophesying." All members are to test everything, and together hold fast to that which is good and abstain from every form of evil. The action is both positive and negative: hold fast to the good and reject the evil.

Today, about the only time the word "discernment" is used is in connection with discerning gifts. Yet nowhere does the New Testament talk about discerning gifts as such. It uses discernment in connection with the will of God. Christians are to discern the truth, what is virtuous, what is good, and how to behave.

One of the gifts of the Holy Spirit is called the discernment of spirits (1 Corinthians 12:7). This is a gift which enables the church to distinguish between a false spirit and a true spirit. In 1 Corinthians 12:3 Paul wrote, "No one speaking by the Spirit of God ever says, 'Jesus be cursed!' " At the same time, "No one can say, 'Jesus is Lord' except by the Holy Spirit." John wrote in his first epistle, "Beloved, do not believe every spirit, but test the spirits to see whether they are of God; for many false prophets have gone out into the world." John's test is similar to Paul's, "By this you know the Spirit of God: every spirit which confesses that Jesus Christ has come in the flesh is of God" (1 John 4:1-3).

The above are key passages that deal with judging, assessing, or discerning. In most of the passages discerning is corporate; occasionally it's personal. Christians are to judge themselves as individuals and are to be judging each other in the congregation.

Now a few observations about discernment.

1. *Discernment is not criticism.* When Peter reported how the Holy Spirit came upon the Gentiles, "the circumcision party criticized him" (Acts 11:2). Criticism is important, depending upon the kind of criticism. But simply to be critical of one another is not discernment in the New Testament sense.

2. A *"hands-off policy" is not discernment.* "Don't say or do anything that will make trouble!" "Don't stir the water." "Keep peace." To cover problems is like putting a Band-Aid on a boil. Paul asked when two brothers were at odds at Corinth, "Can it be that there is no man among you wise enough to decide between members of the brotherhood?" (1 Corinthians 6:5). Hands-off is not discernment.

3. *Partiality inhibits discernment.* James emphasized the need to be impartial. He warned about siding with the rich

person against the poor. Partiality often occurs in congregations. In some congregations whatever certain people say is
"wrong," while what other persons say is "right." Often
issues are decided on the basis of who is in favor and who is
against rather than upon the merits of the case. Such partiality, pitting one against another, inhibits discernment.

4. *Discernment requires biblical awareness.* The believers
at Berea received Paul's preaching with eagerness. However,
they examined the Scriptures daily to see if what he taught
was so. "What does the Bible say?" is an important question.

How one goes to the Scriptures is also important. Too
many try to find a motto or a verse to be used like a rule.
When this happens, words are taken out of context. Standing alone, verses may seem to say one thing; but in their
context, they may say something quite different. It is important to check other passages in the Scripture to find the
whole counsel of God. It is important to try to find out what
Jesus meant, or what Paul meant, to find out what was going
on when a passage emerged or to what it was addressed.

It is important, too, to know what the church has said
about the verse (or verses) under consideration. Often
people claim some "new insight." If they had a historical awareness of Bible interpretation or the development
of doctrine, they would likely find that it was not a new
insight—just new to them. For instance, Victor Werville,
who wrote *Jesus Is Not the Son of God,* claims to have come
to new insights through his own study. The fact is he has not
said anything new, only what has been consistently rejected
by the church for nearly 2,000 years.

In the *New International Version,* 1 Corinthians 4:6 is
beautifully translated, "Now, brothers, I have applied these
things to myself and Apollos for your benefit so that you
may learn from us the meaning of the saying, 'Do not go be-

yond what is written.' " This is a good principle: "Do not go beyond what is written."

5. *Discernment requires the guidance of the Holy Spirit.* A key passage is 1 Corinthians 2:9, 10. Unfortunately, this has been used as a funeral sermon, even though it has no connection with life after death. In fact, Isaiah 64:4 asks Yahweh to come down from heaven to help people see what He has done on earth. "What no eye has seen, nor ear heard, nor the heart of man conceived, what God has prepared for those who love him" does not refer to heaven. In 1 Corinthians 2:9 the point is made that the people of this age do not understand the wisdom of God. The rulers did not understand, for if they had they would not have "crucified the Lord of glory." But God has revealed this through the Spirit. "For the Spirit searches everything, even the depths of God." The Holy Spirit knows the heart and mind of God, and He reveals God's will and way to His people. Paul adds, "Now we have received not the spirit of the world, but the Spirit which is from God, that we might understand the gifts bestowed on us by God." Instead of the word "gifts," the NIV translates it "spiritual things." Discernment requires the guidance of the Holy Spirit.

6. *Discernment requires brotherly love.* In writing about judging, James quoted Leviticus 19:18 and Jesus (Matthew 22:37-39; Mark 12:31), "You shall love your neighbor as yourself," and then added that "in judgment, followers of Jesus are to be merciful" (James 2:8-13).

In Romans 14:1-22 Paul dealt with issues needing discernment—like eating meat and vegetables and observing holy days. Paul made the point that being or not being a vegetarian is a side issue. Bickering and fussing means that Christians are no longer walking in love. Believers are to pursue peace and mutual upbuilding (v. 19). Discernment enables believers to live in harmony with one another (Romans 15:5, 6).

7. *Discernment is done under the searching eye of God.* The New Testament view is this. Christians have received salvation. Today is a day of decision and discernment, because all are moving to the "day of Christ." It's as though Christians are living at the intersection of the cross and the return. Right now, today, they are discerning what the will of God is and are striving for God's approval. Today Christians can discern, through the Spirit and through the Scriptures, what God's will is. What is approved now will be approved in judgment. (This is close to the idea of the kingdom already, but not yet.) Christians can discern now what is required in the day of Christ, and can do now what will be approved then. To discern the will of God now and do it is to be approved. That is why Paul wrote, "It is not the man who commends himself that is accepted, but the man whom the Lord commends"—that is, the one who is discerning now and living in the light of the requirements of the day of Christ (2 Corinthians 10:18).

This brings us to Ephesians 5:7-15, "Try to learn what is pleasing to the Lord." In other words, "Try to discern what is pleasing to the Lord."

"Walk," Paul wrote in that context, "as children of light. Walk as wise men, making the most of the time, because the days are evil."

Appendix

Affirming Our Faith in Word and Deed

We Affirm . . .

1. **The Centrality of Jesus Christ**
   Our faith must have a focus that will conform us to the image of God's Son.
2. **The Primacy of God's Kingdom**
   Our faith should be lived triumphantly as we experience now a foretaste of our future hope.
3. **The Visibility of the Church**
   Our faith needs to be confirmed and confronted by a community of faithful believers.
4. **The Wholeness of Salvation**
   Our faith can be a practical reality in all relationships and spheres of activity.
5. **The Practice of Faith**
   Our faith must retain its integrity while it also becomes credible to the world.

The Mennonite Church in North America, after some 300 years of experience in the New World, has reached a point where it is necessary to reflect again on basic affirmations of faith. The changes in society, the move by many Mennonites from social isolation to involvement in most aspects of North American society, and the coming of peoples from a wide range of cultural and ethnic backgrounds into the church

Reprinted by permission from *Affirming Our Faith in Word and Deed*, copyright © 1978 by Mennonite Publishing House, Scottdale, Pa. 15683.

have created new relationships, new insights, new problems, and new temptations. The move from rural, agricultural roots to urban, professional settings has lessened the cohesive community awareness of many. It has brought diversity of interests and occupations. It has challenged the faith, as questions arose from new knowledge and endeavors. The church itself has too often sought respectability and acceptance rather than obedience and service whatever the consequences. Thus, the traditional forms of faith and the structures of the church are challenged by the new experiences.

The present situation has, on one hand, opened to us secular thought and views of other Christian traditions, many of which do not correspond with our historic understandings of faith and life. On the other hand, the historic understandings often seem inadequate to resolve new issues and to hold the church together in the midst of our fragmented, contemporary society. The time has come for our church to take stock of what we have become in the light of our historical roots (who we are) and in the light of the Scriptures (who God's original people were).

An affirmation of faith, when truly accepted, is the occasion for rejoicing and repentance. As a people from many backgrounds, we rejoice in the affirmation of faith which gives us self-identity. "Once you were no people but now you are God's people" (1 Pet. 2:10). But also, we are called to repentance since each new insight into faith is a call to move from where we are to where we must be. An affirmation of faith is an occasion for renewed, courageous witnessing growing out of a new confidence and a new thankfulness (1 Pet. 2:9).

This Statement of Affirmations is based upon our current confessions of faith; *it does not replace them.* Here comprehensiveness is not sought; rather, this is a response to the present situation in our church with its challenges and needs.

1. The Centrality of Jesus Christ

"For no other foundation can any one lay than that which is laid, which is Jesus Christ" (1 Cor. 3:11).

The Anabaptists rediscovered the apostolic concern "to know nothing . . . except Jesus Christ and him crucified" (1 Cor. 2:2) "in order that in everything God may be glorified through Jesus Christ" (1 Pet. 4:11). These spiritual forebears committed themselves to a thoroughgoing pursuit of this principle. The idea of a Christ-centered faith is not only a statement of belief, but also it is a program of obedient action. To be truly Christian is to give oneself completely to the task of seeing Christ formed in all things—from myself, to all people, and to all creation (Eph. 1:22, 23; Col. 1:15-20; Mt. 28:18-20). Salvation is a process by which this is brought about, at all levels, through the work of Jesus Christ. The Bible is the indispensable source of knowledge of the person of Jesus and the shape of His life. The principle of Christ as the center, however, needs definition and application to avoid a partial and incomplete expression of it.

A Christ-centered faith is not a narrowing of a full Christian teaching. To make Jesus Christ the center is to include: A) the depth of God and B) the breadth of divine revelation.

A) God Himself is most fully revealed in Jesus who lived among us (Jn. 1:8; 14:9; Col. 2:9; 2 Cor. 4:6; Heb. 1:3). All of God's relations to the world find their completion in Him. "All the promises of God find their Yes in him" (2 Cor. 1:20).

B) The Old Testament is included in the Christian vision of truth (Mt. 5:17). The great deeds of salvation in Christ's death, resurrection, and ascension are God's accomplishment (Eph. 1:20), and are the outworking of His purposes throughout history (Acts 2:23; Eph. 3:9, 11). God and His self-revelation are best in focus when viewed through Jesus Christ.

It is in a Christ-centered faith that the ministry of the Holy Spirit can best be understood. The Spirit is a gift of the ascended Christ (Acts 2:33) and is His Spokesman (Jn. 16:13, 14). The work of the Spirit brings into fruition the work of Christ in our personal and social existences. The Spirit is the Executor of Christ's will and testament (Gal. 3:14; 5:5, 25; Rom. 8:9-17; 14:17, 18). On one hand, all claims to the Spirit's work and leading must be judged by their harmony with the life and teaching of Jesus. On the other, the way of living that Jesus taught cannot be followed unless the Spirit empowers believers. To be a disciple of Christ is to be molded into His likeness by the ministry of the Spirit from conversion to consummation (2 Cor. 3:18).

The meaning of a Christ-centered faith is further clarified by the insight that the Christian is to be conformed to the image of God's Son (Rom. 8:29). Conformity to the person of Christ involves the whole person—mind, will, emotions, and deeds. To be Christian is to be transformed at every level of being. This conformity needs to express the full meaning and worth of maleness and femaleness. The distinc-

tiveness of each sex as created by God (1 Cor. 11:7-12) will find meaningful ways to complement one another in the body of Christ (Gal.
3:26-28). A Christ-centered faith is not restricted to certain areas of
existence. Christ's control is to be extended to occupation, to leisure-
time activities, to the arts, and to the sciences. A separation of secular
and sacred is not permitted. All of life is under His direction. The only
separation is between believers and the world not submitted to Christ.

A Christ-centered faith is not aimed only at the individual, nor even
at a series of isolated individuals. The full shape of this faith is found in
the body of Christ—which is the church of Christ-shaped persons! No
one can mature in the image of Christ apart from participation in the
church, His body, in which His fullness dwells (1 Cor. 12; Rom. 12;
Eph. 2:15; 4:11-13).

A Christ-centered faith reaches out to encompass all of creation—
not merely our own people, culture, or country. It is a universal faith in
that it sees Christ as the origin and destiny of all creation (Jn. 1:3; Phil.
2:10). This faith is directed to the realization of Christ's universal lordship (Eph. 1:9, 10; 3:10). Thus a Christ-centered faith is expressed in a
community governed by Christ and committed to a universe filled
with Christ (Eph. 1:9, 10, 20-23).

While Christ includes all truth, He also *excludes*. That which is
totally formed by Christ is conformed to Him alone! The concept of
separation from the world means living a Christ-centered life in a
world that is dominated by molding forces which are not Christlike
(Rom. 12:1, 2). When we hold back Christ from control of all of life,
we allow other lords to move into the vacancies. No one truly knows
Christ except he follow Him daily *in all* of life.

2. The Primacy of God's Kingdom

The biblical story centers in the history of a special people who
represent and carry forward God's purposes in obedient response to
His call (Gen. 12:3; Ex. 19:5, 6). God's choice of the few to bless the
many is, in Scripture, called "election." The people of God, who have
Jesus as Lord, are chosen for this momentous task: "You are a chosen
race . . . God's own people, that you may declare the wonderful deeds
of him who called you out of darkness into his marvelous light" (1 Pet.
2:9). To avoid the pride of such an important claim, we must acknowledge that it is God who works in us to will and to do His good
pleasure (Phil. 2:13).

A. The Two Kingdoms

A tension arises when there is a particular people with a special experience of God in the midst of a society which either willfully or unwittingly ignores the will of God. The Bible sees the world divided into two distinct *kingdoms*. The doctrine of the two kingdoms expresses the fundamental difference between the way of God and the way of evil, i.e., opposition to God. We believe that the church is called to an uncompromising stand for the kingdom of God. When it does so, it is marked by righteousness and peace and joy (Rom. 14:17).

The kingdom of God is His rule, and dominion *in effect*. Wherever the will of God is realized, God's kingdom is present. The church demonstrates kingdom reality when it is faithful. The church, however, is a human institution. It is imperfect. Thus, the kingdom is not identical with the church itself.

B. The Kingdom—Already But Not Yet

Where Jesus is (where His way is lived) the kingdom is at work (Lk. 17:21). But the kingdom of God is both a present fact and a future hope. It is realized, in part, whenever God's will is done, but we also look to the day when His kingdom is to be overall (Eph. 1:10; Rev. 11:15; 19:6). We express the true situation when we pray, "Thy kingdom come" (Mt. 6:10). The claim and the right of the kingdom is already established by God's Son in the victory of the cross, the resurrection, and the ascension (Col. 2:15; Eph. 1:20, 21; Rev. 1:5). It will come into full reality at Christ's return (1 Cor. 15:23-28).

We experience the kingdom now, as a foretaste of what will be when the kingdom comes in its fullness. Many characteristics of what kingdom life will be like have already burst in upon us. Participation in the community of love gives us a foretaste of what kingdom love will be in its glory. Today those in the kingdom beat their swords into plowshares—they are peacemakers. The many languages, cultures, and ethnic backgrounds of believers give us a foretaste of the glory before the throne of God (Rev. 5:6-10). There are dimensions of the kingdom *already* within our midst, but there are dimensions *not yet* experienced and for which we wait.

A lack of clarity concerning the "already but not yet" nature of the kingdom has led to claims that are on one hand "too little" and on the other "too much." For example, the "not yet" emphasis has led some to expect "too little," to put off till later what God expects and offers now. To see the Sermon on the Mount as belonging to another time is "too little." Some have given in to a spirit of defeatism before sin. It is true that now we cannot do God's will perfectly, but we reject a spirit of hopelessness, because the power of the Spirit is available in the face of temptation to sin.

The "already" emphasis has led to the extreme of "too much." For example, some claim that physical healing is as available now as forgiveness. The Bible makes clear that though physical healing is available (Jas. 5:15, 16), it is not a necessary part of the present life of every believer (Rom. 8:10, 23; 2 Cor. 12:9, 10). Some claim unconditional security. While we recognize the keeping power of God now, we are still in the midst of the struggle of flesh and Spirit (Gal. 5:17). Now our security rests on faithfulness and dependence on the work of the Holy Spirit (Gal. 5:5).

When we lose sight of that which is "not yet," we accept the standards of the present age. The church is summoned to demonstrate "the world to come" in the present time (1 Pet. 3:9).

C. Kingdom Life

Christians who are faithful to the vision of an "already but not yet" kingdom are *in* but *not of* the world (Jn. 17:16-18). They are sojourners, or pilgrims. They are a witnessing minority in the world. They stand in a world that is hostile to the faith. Inevitably, they suffer (Mt. 5:10, 11; Rom. 8:17, 18; 2 Tim. 3:12; Phil. 1:29; Heb. 13:13, 14). Suffering for Christ is not the pain of what is old and dying being replaced; rather, it is the pain of birth, in that the new order of things is about to appear. Christians take up the cross and follow the Lord into His glorious future (Mk. 8:34), witnessing until that which "is not yet" comes (Heb. 13:13-16), and enduring the suffering of the cross in the power of the resurrection (Phil. 3:10, 11).

3. The Visibility of the Church

The followers of Jesus, the church, are called out of the world and into commitment one to another. They are identifiable because of their life of obedience to God and separation from evil. Thus, the church is visible (Mt. 5:14; 7:15-20; 1 Pet. 2:9-12).

A. The Church Is the Community of Jesus, the Christ

The purposes of God are being carried out in history by a spe-

cial people who are His servants in behalf of the world, which is
the object of His love (Jn. 3:16). In His ministry, Jesus was a
Servant. His followers are also to be servants. "Whoever would be
the greatest among you must be slave of all. For the Son of Man
also came not to be served but to serve, and to give his life as a
ransom for many" (Mk. 10:44, 45). Jesus is both "Servant of the
Lord" and "Lord of the servants."

Insights concerning the nature of the church as the community
of Jesus are found in Matthew 16:13-20.

1. The Church is a Person-Centered Community

"You are the Christ, the Son of the living God" (v. 16). Here is
confirmation of the centrality of the *person* of Christ in the people
of God. Jesus Christ, in what He is and does, draws believers
together into a common fellowship out of which common ideas,
programs, and interests are formed. This indicates that the community is *relational* in nature. To become a member of this community is to come into relationship to Jesus Christ and into relationship with other believers (Eph. 2:13-19). These relationships
are built around a specific truth—Jesus is the Christ, the Son of
God (v. 16, see also 1 Jn. 4:2; 5:1, 12). This makes life in the
church a *confessional one.* Christian living begins in confession
and continues in confession (Rom. 10:9; Mt. 10:32)—the
confession of Christ. Herein also is the root of both worship and
witness—the acclamation of Jesus as Lord. Every act of life is
both worship and witness (Rom. 12:1) when done in Christ's
name.

2. The Church Is a Called-out Community

"Flesh and blood has not revealed this to you, but my Father
who is in heaven. And I tell you . . . I will build my church" (vv.
17, 18). Natural causes and natural means do not create the
church. A Christian community is the work of divine power. Jesus
is the *Builder* of the church. The church cannot be reduced to a
self-controlled and self-perpetuating institution. The true definition of the church is not right theology confessed and correct
ritual practiced. Rather it is a community of faithful persons in
relationship with Christ and with each other, following Him in all
of life.

3. The Church Is an Overcoming Force

"The powers of death shall not prevail against it" (v. 18).

While the church is a spiritual reality, it is no less a visible, earthly, physical reality. Christians are related to specific realities of this world. In the context of this life in the world, the church wrestles against the power of evil, and is committed to establishing the order of God wherever possible. In this order the church is strengthened by the reassuring word of final triumph. That victory, both present and future, is conditioned by her continuing steadfastness.

4. The Church Is a Discerning People

"I will give you the keys of the kingdom of heaven, and whatever you bind on earth shall be bound in heaven, and whatever you loose on earth shall be loosed in heaven" (v. 19). The people of God become a visible community because their life, their actions, and their decisions in this world are interlocked with eternal "actions and decisions." Members commit themselves to wait expectantly in the presence of Jesus Christ to discover together the mind of Christ through the guidance of the Holy Spirit and the Scriptures.

The Lord of the church addresses His people through individuals. Believers, however, test the genuineness of these addresses to see if they are truly the word of Christ (1 Cor. 14:29; 1 Thess. 5:19-22). The authority of the word does not depend on the position of the speaker. Rather, the authority of the word is confirmed by the community which is committed to do the word.

"Binding and loosing" take place within the circle of believers (Mt. 18:15-20). This process of correction and discipline is intended to guard brothers and sisters from loss of faith. In this way the Lord of the church forms visible communities of holy living. The disciplined church is the holy community where the goal of obedience is high, but where the weaknesses of the disciples are confronted by loving concern and offers of forgiveness (Gal. 6:1). Binding and loosing is legitimate only when done "in the name of Christ," that is, in His character and will (Mt. 18:20; Col. 3:17). It is the work of the congregation rather than of a hierarchy controlling the congregation. (Compare the singular "you" and the plural "you" in Matthew 16:19 and 18:18.)

B. The Church Is the Community of the Spirit

The transition from a disciple band in the company of Jesus of Nazareth to the church under the lordship of the exalted Christ changed the form but not the substance of the new community of Christ. The resurrection of Jesus made it possible for Him to be present in a new way, by the Spirit who is the "other Christ" (Jn. 14:16-18; 16:14; Acts 2:33). In the present time, therefore, the true church is defined as a visible company of believers in whose midst Jesus Christ is present *by the Spirit.*

1. The Church Is the Firstfruits of the Spirit

The work of the Spirit is described as firstfruits (Rom. 8:23). As Christ is the firstfruits of those who sleep by reason of His resurrection (1 Cor. 15:20), so Christian believers are firstfruits of the future kingdom of God. The Spirit creates a new order of things in and among them. Believers see themselves as a colony of heaven, a city of God erected in the midst of an unreconstructed world (Mt. 5:14). This community of the Spirit is, in God's intention, a model of the way things will be in the consummation of all things.

2. The Church Demonstrates the Fruit of the Spirit

The fruit of the Spirit is that which characterizes the new person and his/her relationships, in the new order of existence under Christ. The list of the Spirit's fruit (Gal. 5:22, 23) follows closely the virtues in the Sermon on the Mount—love, joy, peace, patience, kindness, goodness, faithfulness, gentleness, self-control. Just as Jesus presupposed that such traits were possible only for the disciple who lives in the Master's presence and who participates in the saving power of the kingdom (Mt. 4:17-25), so also Paul observes that the believer lives in this fashion through the power of the Spirit release in the new Israel of God (Gal. 6:16). There are several aspects of the fruit of the Spirit which are crucial among the people of God:

a) *Love* is the key to all Christian relationships. The self-giving desire for the good of another is what the believer has seen in the Father and the Son, and he passes it on in his own relationships. The specific shape of this love is seen in the servant role—"through love be servants of another" (Gal. 5:13). No characteristic so marks the church as different from the unredeemed society. Paul's insight that freedom is experienced in service to another is incomprehensible to the unregenerate mind—and unfortunately also to many confessing believers. Other virtues such as patience, kindness, and gentleness are extensions of this basic outlook.

The church gives visible expression to its commitment to serving love by the observance of foot washing. This symbolic act, commanded by the Lord Himself (Jn. 13) is a reminder that disciples are servants just as Jesus was a servant. This simple act challenges the believer to display love in service in all of life.

b) *Joy* is the characteristic attitude and mood of the new life. It is not mere coincidence that the earliest church broke into joy and praise at the realization that Jesus had been raised by the Father (Lk. 24:52) and that Jesus had poured out the Spirit who gives a shower of heavenly foretastes, pledges of the final establishment of the heavenly order (Acts 2:46; 3:19-21). In the same vein, Jesus pronounced blessedness and joy upon the disciples who had cast their fortune with the new work of God in Jesus (Mt. 5:3-12). Suffering was only a confirmation of the blessedness, not its negation.

c) *Peace* is the description of the order of things when the will of God is in effect. Each thing is in its proper place and each person is in a proper relationship with God, neighbor, and world. The experience of peace in a world of chaos is a foretaste of the peaceable kingdom of biblical prophecy. For this reason believers pursue peace and dedicate their efforts to bringing it to realization (Ps. 34:14; Mt. 5:9; Jas. 3:18; 1 Pet. 3:11). Witness and service for peace stand, then, at the heart of our faith. Negatively, it means refusing to participate in the military or to exercise a vengeful spirit (Rom. 12:19). Positively, it means to follow Christ in peacemaking (Mt. 5:9). This is a work of the Spirit among and through believers.

3. The Church is Gifted by the Holy Spirit

The Holy Spirit distributes gifts to the church (1 Cor. 12:4-11, 27-31; Rom. 12:4-8; Eph. 4:11-16). These gifts enable each member to contribute to the well-being and growth of the entire body (1 Cor. 14:12). The Spirit gives gifts to men and women as He wills.

It is in a proper understanding of the gifted community that our concept of authority among believers emerges. Here a course is steered between the democracy of majority rule and the authoritarianism of minority rule. The gifts of the spirit remove the idea that everyone is equally able to play every role. The gifts of the Spirit also remove the tendency for a representative elite to decide things "too difficult for the whole body." In a gifted community, every member has equal access to God (Gal. 3:28) and, therefore, may at some particular time be God's channel of communication to the community (1 Cor. 14:29-33). There is a need for structure and for order in leadership (Heb. 13:17), but these should reflect the actual distribution of gifts. Gifting by the Spirit should encourage believers to submit themselves one to another as servants (Eph. 5:21; 1 Pet. 5:2).

The authority of the Bible in the church emerges at this point. The Bible is the result of the gifts of prophecy and apostleship (those who saw the Lord) by which the Holy Spirit has given guidance of a once-for-all character to the church. These documents, therefore, provide an accurate picture of Jesus Christ who is our authority (Jn. 5:39, Lk. 24:27). They reveal truth by which believers test but not displace the living voice of the Spirit today. The uniqueness of these writings is indicated by their God-inspired character (1 Tim. 3:16).

4. The Church Is Empowered by the Holy Spirit

The work of the Spirit is directed toward giving the new community power for the task of mission. The church is not made a power among the powers of the world. Rather, the church is given power to confront centers of power in economics, in government, and in religious establishments (Mk. 13:11; Acts 4:29-31; 19:23-27). The power of the witness consists in being true followers of Jesus Christ, the group which anticipates the heavenly city in the world (Mt. 5:14).

The mission of the disciple community has a unique power which is in harmony with its inner life:

a) Mission begins in *demonstration.* The very life Christians live, as an alternative to that of a fallen world, is a witness, simply in its being present in the world (1 Pet. 2:12; 3:1, 2). In Jesus' ministry the works of power demonstrated the presence of God's kingdom. In the church the works of the Spirit (see above) are signs of eternal life at work. Therefore, ministries of service and peace are essential to being God's people in mission. They are acts of blessing for mankind, and point the world to the new life in God's kingdom.

b) Mission moves to *explanation*. The most effective witness is explaining something that has been demonstrated. At Pentecost the first evangelistic sermon was an explanation of the display of Spirit power. The importance of explanation lies in the fact that good works can be variously interpreted by the observer.

c) Mission involves *declaration* (announcement). Gifted persons come forward to declare to the world the will of God, the way of salvation, and the results of disobedience. This prophetic ministry is related to the community where the life that is offered is observable.

Thus mission is a function of the Spirit. Mission is a movement from the gathered life of the community where worship, exhortation, and empowering takes place, to the scattered life in the world where spiritual power is released in acts of love and in words of liberation.

4. The Wholeness of Salvation

Salvation has a wide meaning in the Bible. It includes all the gracious acts of God for man in both spiritual and material realms. It includes the present benefits as well as the future. Salvation is a process. Salvation is individual and corporate. Salvation is simple, yet complex. Salvation provides liberation for spirit and body. Salvation provides a new nature created in the image of God (Gen. 1:26, 27; Eph. 4:24; Col. 3:10). The first experience of salvation makes us desire the completion of it, and assures us that this will indeed be the case (Rom. 8:24).

In recent times we have been influenced by a view that limits salvation: salvation is an act whereby God gains control of the soul and purifies it from sin, so that when the person dies or the world is destroyed, the soul will dwell with God in another sphere called heaven. This is not the biblical view of salvation, of man (body and soul are not against one another), nor of the future (the new "world" will be a new heaven *and* a new earth). This definition is *wrong* because it is *incomplete*, not because what it says is incorrect.

Salvation viewed in the framework of a Christ-centered faith, the two kingdoms, and a visible church maintains an all-inclusiveness. The spiritual pilgrimage of a believing disciple involves various stages. These are not consecutive, rather they are a constellation of experiences that compose the meaning of salvation:

A. Repentance and Conversion

The new life begins in a *new* way of seeing life and oneself. It is a change of mind. When a person is offered an alternative way of life, he is free to "change his/her mind." When Jesus brought the kingdom of heaven (of God) and demonstrated it, people were encouraged to repent and believe the good news (Mk. 1:15). When the believer acknowledges the error of the old life and embraces the new, this is called *repentance*. When the believer identifies with the source of salvation (God), with the Master (Jesus), and with fellow believers (the disciples), this change is called *conversion*.

B. Forgiveness and Reconciliation

God's forgiveness and His desire for reconciliation with His children are expressed in the parable of the loving father fully accepting the prodigal son and joyfully restoring him to his place within the father's family (Lk. 15:11-32). This does not mean that sin and disobedience are overlooked. It is necessary that right relationships be restored with a righteous God.

The fact of sin in our lives creates a two-directional barrier: a barrier between us and God, and a barrier between people. This barrier runs counter to God's purpose of "uniting all things in him" (Eph. 1:10). As sinners (Rom. 3:23), we are unable to tear down this two-directional barrier ourselves. It is God through Christ who reconciles us to Himself (2 Cor. 5:19). In the death of Jesus a covering and removal of sin were made possible (Rom. 3:23-26). Furthermore, the blood of Christ has broken down the dividing wall of hostility and has made one those who were divided (Eph. 2:13-16).

By faith we are reconciled to God and receive the power of forgiveness. It is God's forgiveness which enables us to forgive others as we have been forgiven.

C. Regeneration and New Birth

The change that Jesus Christ brings to the believer is so thoroughgoing that it is described as passing from death to life, from one kingdom to another, or as a new birth (Col. 1:13). The new birth means the passage from nonexistence to existence in spiritual relationship (Jn. 3)—to the position of sons and daughters in the family of God. The same change is also described as a "new creation" (2 Cor. 5:17). This suggests not only personal transformation, but also a change of social context—environment. This is not removal from earthly existence; rather, it involves identification with the family of God, the church, where the new order of things—the new creation—is already being experienced.

D. "In Christ"

A comprehensive way to describe salvation is "in or with Christ." The disciple identifies with the Master, lives the experiences of the Master, in whose presence he constantly remains. Jesus is the model for Christian experience as well as its Giver (Rom. 8:29).

Two observances of the church, baptism and breaking of bread, remind us of the wholeness of salvation. They remind us of dying and rising with Christ and putting on Christ. These are not mysterious hidden occurrences. Rather, believers place Jesus Christ at the head of their lives, so that the character of Jesus and the historical events of His death and resurrection are brought to bear on their personal experience (Gal. 2:20; Rom. 6; Mk. 8:34-38; Phil. 2:5 ff.; 1 Pet. 4:1). "For as many of you as were baptized into Christ have put on Christ ... you are all one in Christ Jesus" (Gal. 3:27, 28).

1. Baptism

Water baptism is the confession that salvation has begun in one's life. It is also the expression of personal commitment to Jesus. At the same time the congregation observes and acknowledges that the Spirit indeed has worked in the life of the one baptized.

The person being baptized looks forward to the disciple life, and promises to be faithful till death. Historically, the one being baptized puts all possessions at the disposal of the community, in recognition that all of life belongs to Jesus Christ, and that life is a stewardship. At the same time members of the congregation commit themselves to that person, offering counsel, care, and help in time of need.

Baptism marks the point of identification with the visible body of Christ, apart from which the full stature of Christ is unattainable (Eph. 4:13). A baptismal service which does not provide a relationship to the visible church does not fully symbolize the meaning of the act.

Since baptism is a mark of conversion and identification with Christ and His body, it is properly administered only to those who are capable of making a decision to be a disciple of Jesus. Baptism is for those who are ready to devote themselves to discipling in a local community of faith where the life of discipleship and the activities of admonition and encouragement are part of the common life. The age of readiness for baptism is a matter needing careful discernment on the part of the congregation. In general, any sincere requests for baptism should be honored as long as the candidate is able to perceive clearly the implications of the request and is capable of living a life of discipleship.

2. Breaking Bread

Breaking bread reminds us how God both initiated and works out His whole salvation, as it recalls the death of Jesus, reviews its benefits, and proclaims the good news till He comes again.

Just as baptism assumes a visible community with which to be identified, so breaking bread assumes a visible body—the congregation or community of God whose Head is Jesus Christ.

Those who break bread in remembrance of the broken body of Jesus Christ, and those who drink the one drink in remembrance of the shed blood must be united beforehand in the one body of Christ (1 Cor. 11:17-32). Those who partake examine themselves (1 Cor. 11:28). They are also open to their brothers and sisters for admonition and correction because they take seriously the warnings of Paul about drinking the cup of the Lord and the cup of devils (1 Cor. 10:21). In the historic view of breaking bread, neither the nature nor the meaning of the bread and cup, nor the status of the one officiating is the point of concern. The concern is with the community—those who take part, that all should share the one calling of God, the one faith, the one baptism, the one spirit, and thus be made one loaf together (1 Cor. 10:17).

E. Occupation

The call to discipleship is the Christian's *vocation*. Vocation, however, is never isolated from *occupation*—lifework. In fact, God's call to salvation is stated as being for the purpose of doing a work for God (Acts 9:15). This is the dimension of faith which needs emphasis today when spirituality is often reserved for religious spheres of activity, and when members are moving into an increasingly wide range of occupations. All realms of life are under Christ's lordship, and are part of His saving purpose (see above). Thus, all areas of human activity are potentially meaningful areas of work for the believer—*on condition that they are consistent with the character*

and purpose of God in Christ. Since the servant style is characteristic
of disciple life, those occupations with a strong service dimension.
are particularly appropriate.   •

F. The Christian Way of Life
   1. Simplicity
   Our whole life must witness to the healing and wholesomeness
that salvation brings. The new style of serving, loving, discipleship finds application in relationships to nature and to neighbor.

   The Christian is a steward of God's good earth, of possessions,
and of time. The establishment of justice and peace in relationship with others is also of great concern. The simple life avoids
both pride and greed.

   2. Piety
   An important result of salvation is corporate and personal
piety. Regular, disciplined study of the Word combined with
prayer that listens for God to speak, enables one to discover the
depths of self and the depths of Christ. The Christian also needs
the challenge of the group; the group needs the insights that
come from individual reflection and prayer.

   Often when the disciplines of personal and corporate piety are
not cultivated, persons will long for a subjective experience with
Christ, but will look to others to fill that need (the super-preacher,
thrilling teacher, or sparkling testimony and music). This may
weaken the overall strength of the congregation and open the
way for ambition, competition, and manipulation in the fellowship.

5. The Practice of Faith

Both the content of faith and the expression of faith are essential in
practical living. The process by which faith is kept new, passed on to
children, shared with the world, and adapted to new situations must
be guided by the creativeness of the Holy Spirit and fulfilled through
the obedience of faith in the life of the church. Perhaps we are
threatened more by a breakdown in the processes of our common life
than by an erosion of our unique doctrines. Here are some processes
which need our response.

A. Celebrating
   A *faith that is openly expressed is lively and grows in meaning for
the believer.* The experience of God's people in every age shows that

the telling of the deeds of God is a spontaneous and meaningful act, beneficial to speaker and listener (Mal. 3:16). It clarifies and confirms the understanding and commitments of the speaker; it challenges or confirms the experiences of the hearer. The confession of the mouth is a confirmation to the heart. Faith that is not affirmed will not remain firm.

The community of faith will want to provide a variety of opportunities for collective and individual statements of faith by all its members. As the New Testament shows, these expressions will range from formal recitations of the basic tenets of faith (see 1 Tim. 3:16) to spontaneous, testimonials in worship—"a hymn, a lesson, a revelation, a tongue, or an interpretation" (1 Cor. 14:26). Sometimes, avoiding set patterns and encouraging variety will allow more persons to participate comfortably and meaningfully.

B. Educating

A *faith that is deeply understood and personally appropriated affects changes at the center of one's person; such faith is both lived and shared.* The personal commitment of members to a believers' church cannot be coerced. It is a voluntary matter. The transmission of faith is a primary concern. The people of God cannot depend upon forms of education by which they became members of secular society or even of the natural family. Education in the congregation is under the direction of the Lord of the church, as the Holy Spirit teaches, guides, and gives gifts so that all persons may grow toward maturity in Christ.

What does this mean for the handing on of faith from generation to generation in a voluntary church? First, there is the possibility that our biological children will not be our spiritual offspring. Christian parents can provide opportunities for faith to be learned, but *they cannot guarantee that children will accept the faith.* Parents must avoid both false guilt and unspiritual compulsion in relating to children.

Second, education in Christian contexts is primarily by example, explained by word. Jesus transmitted His cause by selecting a group of disciples who would demonstrate the message along with their telling of it. Jesus did what He saw the Father do (Jn. 5:19, 20); the disciple is to do as he has seen Jesus do (Jn. 13:15). The new believer looks to the example of the spiritually more mature (Phil. 4:8, 9; Heb. 6:12, 13:7). For a spiritual community that takes its life model from discipleship, learning by example is expected: " . . . but everyone when he is fully taught will be like his teacher" (Lk. 6:40).

Third, the symbols of brotherhood life are important. A church which emphasizes visible, concrete obedience in all of life will develop acts and forms which will remind the members of its convictions. Jesus Himself gave a symbol of entrance into the community—baptism; a symbol of fellowship in His presence—breaking bread (see above); and a symbol of brotherly love and service—foot washing. Other symbols have been observed on biblical grounds—the prayer veiling, the kiss of charity, anointing with oil, and laying on of hands.

Several guidelines are clear in regard to symbols: 1) symbols are inevitable in a religious, social institution like the church. We cannot express faith in life without them. Therefore, the church must use seriousness in their preservation or modification. Apathy and change by default are not virtues. 2) Symbols are not the reality of faith, but are the expression of it. Therefore, symbols are secondary. The reality guarantees the symbol, but the symbol does not guarantee the reality. 3) Symbols can, and will, come and go, but the essence of faith still remains. The symbols of universal application based on Scripture, however, are a differing matter.

C. Serving

Faith is expressed in love and service, in word and deed. Serving is the Christian's response to God's grace. Because salvation is more than a private matter, it becomes salt and light and leaven, visibly demonstrated in the world. Jesus modeled serving. He went about the cities and towns teaching . . . preaching . . . healing . . . and serving (Mk. 10:46-52). He demonstrated that loving servanthood is an alternative kind of power—more powerful than hostility and more convincing than force.

Following Christ's example, His servants model a new humanity. They demonstrate alternatives to bondage, and offer life renewed in Christ. This offer is extended to everyone (Jn. 3:16). As the Father showers rain on the just and the unjust (Mt. 5:43-48), and as Jesus showed no partiality (Mk. 7:24-30), so Christ's servants do not restrict their acts of love to a particular group of people. Jesus' forgiveness of His executioners was an extraordinary manifestation of this kind of love, given with extravagance even to those who did not ask for it. In this is revealed love, that while we were sinners and enemies, Christ died for us (Rom. 5:8-11).

Christ's servants go into the world fully aware that their values differ sharply from society: 1) Christ's servants go in the spirit of love as advocates for the victims of injustice. In contrast, worldly servants tend to lord it over others and make them feel the full weight of their authority (Mk. 10:42, 43). 2) Christ's servants consciously challenge the values of society. Through creative resistance they consciously separate themselves from and witness against the power structures of the prevailing culture which perpetually deny to many people basic human rights. 3) Christ's servants show another way. They offer the new community, made possible through Christ, where persons are of higher value than property, and where property is used to serve the common good (Acts 5:32-37). 4) Christ's servants confront both personal and social sins. They offer a gospel that has both personal and social implications (Eph. 2:17-22). To offer one without the other is to present a half gospel, which is not a gospel at all. The good news includes both.

Thus Christ's servants invite individuals to Christ. They are concerned about individual morality and personal sins such as pride, lust, greed, lack of love. Christ's servants also confront any evil which threatens God's creation—the waste and misuse of God's natural resources (air, water, land, energy). They confront the militarization of society, the overconsumption of the rich, the exploitation of the poor (Mt. 6:24), the oppression of unscrupulous landlords, the neglect of prisoners (Heb. 13:3), and the bigotry of racial bias and discrimination.

Christ's servants do not accept the world as it is. They constantly extend the invitation to all persons to come to Christ, and to participate in His kingdom, the new order that is beginning now. To witness for Christ as servants is risky, and leads to suffering. The cross has demonstrated that through suffering love, evil is confronted and overcome.

D. Proclaiming

Faith is to be proclaimed; its integrity must be preserved. The faith of a disciple church becomes credible to the world when it is illustrated in believers' lives. Faith retains its credibility to the church when it sees the results of its proclamation in changed lives. The healthiest atmosphere for personal, disciple growth is in a growing church, where: 1) new members are being born into kingdom existence; 2) where members serve one another and minister to those in need; 3) where persons are growing in Christlikeness. Where no "new births" and no witness and service occur, that community faces extinction in the next generation and gradual paralysis and decay in the present.

Proclamation provides many benefits for the community itself. Problems of relationships within the fellowship are kept in proper perspective when the primary tasks of proclamation and of service unite the fellowship in common task. Furthermore, the process of stating the faith in the public arena helps to keep faith honest and intelligible in the world in which we are called to represent Christ's kingdom. The church's faithfulness is worked out between the two tasks of preserving the integrity of faith and of propagating the faith. Neither task can be effectively carried out without the other.

The centrality of Christ is not an "exlusive" conviction of Anabaptist/Mennonite faith. That this is shared with other Christians results in a basis for discussion and interaction. This leads hopefully to increased consistency of faith for each group, and thus common ground for fellowship. The search for unity among Christians is based on the conformity to the mind of Christ. Our family of faith has recovered and discovered unique implications of the centrality of Christ. This gives us something unique to contribute to the larger family. In fact, it is only in maintaining our self-identity that we can make a larger contribution.

E. Discerning

Faith must be tested for genuineness and applied to new situations of life. Few questions of the believers' church are more crucial than that of the process by which we deal with decision-making in matters of faith. We tend to seek protective conditions where the labor and risk of evaluating and correcting are avoided. Often authority is delegated to a few who decide, or we create isolated communities where the cultural and doctrinal expressions of one generation can simply be perpetuated in a static situation. The appearance of preservation is an illusion. It is done at the cost of maturity in each believer, and at the cost of a vital witness to a way of life that is a visible alternative to that of general society.

The church, to remain true to herself, must be on the move in a changing world. The church cannot stand still. The comforting thought that all things are the same as before is the first step to the loss of the first love. Only a living faith that goes out to meet the future will avoid the deviant path or the imperceptible drift. "Keeping the faith" is possible only in testing, correcting, adapting, and growing to meet new situations or in response to new understandings. Freezing words, actions, and expressions of our faith does not preserve the faith. An open stance to faith is not "too risky." Risk cannot be removed from true faith. There is risk in change and in no change.

Finally, here are two areas in which discernment is needed:

1. The Relation Between *Faith and Culture*

Culture is the external expression of a people's life. A disciple church which stresses obedience in all of life faces the issues of how faith relates to the cultural aspects of life. Cultures of this world differ and change. For this reason, discernment is constantly needed as the gospel penetrates new cultural settings and as old cultures change. The gospel cannot avoid a cultural dress, but it is obligated to demonstrate its own unique quality in and through cultural forms—in conformity to Christ.

In cultural matters testing and checking are necessary. History shows and contemporary experience indicates that the cultural expressions of Mennonite faith have not always developed in consistency with our Anabaptist vision. This split between the vision and the reality within our congregations must be carefully assessed. As long as we live in the present age, our imperfections will cause differences between the vision and the reality. But the vision both corrects our failures and helps us to move in the proper direction.

2. The Relation Between *Scripture and Tradition*

Mennonites have always been clear that Scripture is above tradition. But in practice this has not been clear. Many are fearful that the way of our fathers (tradition) might need modification. For them change appears to be unfaithfulness at the most, and disrespect at the least. Yet, since Scripture is the greatest authority, this conclusion is inevitable: faithfulness means readiness to correct what we do in light of clearer knowledge of God's Word. Each new generation must discover this for itself, and be open to new light that might correct or enrich our biblical faith.

Finally, there is no substitute for a living, dynamic relationship to Jesus Christ in the present moment. However, the present must be guided by the truth from the past (Scripture illuminated but not interpreted by tradition) and the hope toward which we move (1 Jn. 3:2, 3). *A church that looks for a city to come is faithful only if it is on the move.*

"This is a faithful saying, and these things I will that thou affirm constantly, that they which have believed in God might be careful to maintain good works" (Tit. 3:8).

Scripture Index

Old Testament

New Testament

Paul M. Lederach, Scottdale, Pennsylvania, is an ordained minister in the Mennonite Church, presently a member of Allegheny Mennonite Conference, serving as an overseer and chairman of the Ministerial committee.

He was field secretary of the Mennonite Commission for Christian Education (1952-59); editor of the Herald Graded Sunday School Series (1952-61); director of the Curriculum Development and Service Department of Mennonite Publishing House, Scottdale, Pennsylvania (1961-69), administered its Congregational Literature Division (1970-73), and was executive director of The Foundation Series curriculum (1973-78). He was president of the Mennonite Board of Education from 1964 to 1971. More recently he chaired the Affirmation of Faith Task Force of the General Assembly of the Mennonite Church.

Lederach received his BA from Goshen College, Goshen, Indiana; his ThB from Goshen Biblical Seminary; his MRE from Eastern Baptist Theological Seminary, Philadelphia, Pennsylvania; and his DEd from Southwestern Baptist Theological Seminary, Fort Worth, Texas. He studied at the University of Pittsburgh under a Religious Education Association Lilly Foundation · Post-Doctoral Empirical Research Training Fellowship (1965-66).

He is author of *Learning to Teach* (1964); *Reshaping the Teaching Ministry* (1968); *Living with Kindergarten Children* (1970); *Mennonite Youth* (1971), *The Spiritual Family and the Biological Family* (1973), and *Teaching in the Congregation* (1979).

Paul M. and Mary (Slagell) Lederach are members of the Scottdale Mennonite Church. They are parents of four children: James, Judith, Deborah, and Rebecca. Lederach is self-employed in insurance and real estate.